NORTHWEST STYLE

NORTHWEST STYLE

Interior Design and Architecture in the Pacific Northwest

TEXT BY ANN WALL FRANK

PHOTOGRAPHS BY MICHAEL MATHERS

CHRONICLE BOOKS
SAN FRANCISCO

First paperback edition published in 2003 by
Chronicle Books LLC.

Manufactured in Hong Kong
Book and cover design by Lucy Nielsen
Cover photography by Michael Mathers
Typeset in Democratica, Futura, Minion, and Syntax

Library of Congress Cataloging-in-Publication Data:

Frank, Ann Wall.
Northwest Style: interior design and architecture in the Pacific Northwest / Ann Wall Frank ; photography by Michael Mathers.
204 p. 25.2 x 25.2 cm.
Includes bibliographical references and index.
ISBN 0-8118-4149-9
1. Architecture, Domestic—Northwest, Pacific. 2. Architecture, Modern—20th century—Northwest, Pacific. 3. Interior decoration—Northwest, Pacific. I. Mathers, Michael H. II. Title.
728'.09795—dc21 CIP
99-17976

Distributed in Canada by Raincoast Books
9050 Shaughnessy Street
Vancouver, BC V6P 6E5

10 9 8 7 6 5 4 3 2 1

Chronicle Books LLC
85 Second Street
San Francisco, CA 94105

www.chroniclebooks.com

Dedicated to my dear sister, Linda, whose wisdom, humor, encouragement, and wellspring of love keep me inspired. —AWF

To my parents and their wonderful style. —MHM

ACKNOWLEDGMENTS

I could not have written this book without the support, guidance, insight, direction, and encouragement of so many people. I want to thank, first of all, the homeowners featured in this book, who so graciously opened their wonderful homes to share with readers. Thanks to the Seattle and Portland public libraries for their cheerful and patient assistance with research and to the Portland and Seattle American Institute of Architects for steering me in the right direction. Countless individuals also helped me brainstorm about this vast fabulous contrast that is the Northwest so that I could begin writing about it. They also fetched me lattes! I also wish to thank Sheri Okubo for helping with fact checking and Erin Malecha for her eagle eye. Billye Turner, Patricia Williams, Bette Sinclair, Kathy Wetherell, Marilynn Jensen, Kathy Rensch, Dennis Burns, Marie Bailey, and Margo Jacobsen are just a few of the people who put me on the track to exciting homes. Thanks to Daphne Cooluris for reminding me that style—inside and out—is both generous and brave. To Sara Perry for introducing me to Chronicle Books, to my editors, Christina Wilson and Leslie Jonath, and to my wonderful agent, Jeremy Solomon, for his constant guidance and support. Finally, and most important, thanks to my husband, Jeff, for his patience, love, and computer savvy and for cheerfully eating popcorn for dinner more times than he wishes to recount.

Page 1: Biben/Bosley Vacation House.
Page 2: Paulk House.
Page 3: Orcas Island Escape.
Right: Gardner House.
Page 6: Stevens House.
Page 7: (right bottom) Hathaway House, (right top) Stevens House.
Page 9: Hubbard House.

CONTENTS

INTRODUCTION

Try to pin a style on us, and the people of the Pacific Northwest will be the first to throw it off. We like to think of ourselves as transcending labels, as an independent breed of mavericks and iconoclasts, in love with the wild and perfect beauty of the place, charged with keeping chaste the last virgin on the planet. As a cult of leisure and experts on informality, we share a passion for the outdoors and seek endless ways to worship nature: gardening, sailing, hiking, skiing, camping, and fishing.

It is this defiance to description that makes the Pacific Northwest so wonderful, if not contradictory: casual, stylish, provocative, indifferent, egalitarian, snobbish, progressive, and provincial, we are quiet about our money, loud about our land. Salmon treaties are as likely to make headlines in the major dailies as the latest political scandal, and we would rather admit to a bank heist than to not recycling.

Our environmental sensitivity has earned us a national reputation as a bunch of nature-loving recyclers and rain-soaked bibliophiles who require an act of congress before we cut down a tree. All true. But with more than 78 percent of our land mass (in both Washington and Oregon) in forests, trees are a vital part of our economy, the symbol of our spirit and also of our discontent. The Northern spotted owl incites its share of heated debates held over a glass or two of microbrew, and land-use laws have incited their share of infamous barroom brawls.

Running a high fever over nature seems justified, though, to anyone who has ever glimpsed the region's beauty. This rugged corner of the world consisting of Washington, Oregon, and lower British Columbia is a vast, lush overstatement. Pristine rivers, gem-colored lakes, snow-capped mountains, primeval temperate rainforests, fragrant orchards, and the stark relief of a high-desert silhouette envelop the big cities, small towns, sleepy villages, and busy harbors that lead to the Pacific Ocean.

Despite rumors that to adapt to all the rain, the natives have grown webbed feet, the climate is moderate, allowing for a fecundity of growth and a strong agricultural economy, from fruit to wheat to mint. In spring the landscape is riotous: cherry trees, poppies, lilacs, rhododendrons, and roses bloom at once, carpeting the hillsides and valleys with color. Mountain meadows blaze with wildflowers, and fragrant orchards are dense with succulent blossoms. Nestled under the mountains, in the fir-covered plateaus of the Mount Hood wilderness area, grow the Northwest's delicacy, morel mushrooms. Every year small battles are waged over the musky, spongy, faintly sweet wild morels as hunters and gatherers face off in their pursuit of the forest's bounty.

All this green means that we take more rain than any but the most dreary of souls could find tolerable. Even the intrepid explorer Merriwether Lewis became bored and cranky when he forged the mouth of the Columbia River in search of the fabled Northwest Passage. He wrote in his journal that he couldn't fix longitude and latitude to start a decent map. "I am mortifyed at not having it in my power to make more celestial observations since we have been at Fort Clatsop, but such has been the state of the weather that I have found it utterly impracticable." Thus, in perhaps that first recorded complaint of seasonal affective disorder, Merriwether summed up our winters, most of spring, and a chunk of the fall.

But not *all* of the Northwest is wet, soggy, and gray. East of the Cascade mountain range lies Oregon's high-desert country, where open lands are dotted with craggy peaks, ponderosa pines, silky wheatlands, and lakes that fill with pure glacial waters in colors of apple green, aquamarine, and milky jade. Washington's Inland Empire, with Spokane as its population hub, is a rich agricultural region where rows of crops line up like a brilliant green corduroy patch on Eden's pocket. Among other things, the best cherries in the country grow here. And like Oregon east of the Cascades, eastern Washington is hot and dry. Most of the precipitation comes in the form of snow.

Northwest people are as diverse as their landscape. Perhaps due to the melding of fur traders, fishermen, gamblers, gold seekers, timber barons, and pioneers, the spirit of adventure runs rampant.

The white wood fence, with its straight boards and simple turnings, is an adaptation of the Queen Anne style. An earthenware jug placed between the arbors fills with rainwater for thirsty birds.

Innovative, creative, and iconoclastic, we are a study in irreverence. Visitors claim that we are extremely friendly and polite—they just don't know what we're unfriendly and impolite *about.* Oregon's governor from 1966 to 1974, the relentlessly straight-talking Tom McCall, urged people to visit, adding on, "but for heaven's sake, don't come to live here." For years his quip served as Oregon's insider motto and spawned a cottage industry of "un-greeting cards" and other "keep out" paraphernalia.

Despite a certain intractability (we cannot seem to lose the idea of wearing jeans to the ballet), we remain a wellspring of innovation. Oregon led the country in recycling consciousness by introducing the bottle bill, and Washington's curbside recycling program has become a model for the nation. Seattle celebrates an annual "ride your bike to work day," where, rain or shine, the collective pedals in earnest. Portland's Yellow Bike Project encourages people to pick up one of the free bikes scattered around the rose city, pedal to their destination, and then leave their bike for the next person. Sometimes the bikes are stolen or vandalized: the city just gets more yellow bikes. After all, Portland's a city designed for using your feet, not your engine.

We gave the country (and the planet) Microsoft, microbrew, and the culinary genius of James Beard. A running cult was spawned in Eugene, beginning with a shoe whose sole was first created in a waffle iron. Seattle brought the grunge movement to the street scene and remains one of the best sources of vintage fashion in the nation. Billions of dollars have floated in on the ubiquitous microchip, Starbucks made coffee a sacrament, and Portland made bookstores into shrines.

The arts have always been important to the region, despite the struggle to boot aside provincialism in favor of exploration. Seattle and Vancouver, British Columbia, have popular symphonies, and Seattle has a nationally acclaimed opera. The Northwest School of the 1950s gave birth to the much-collected artworks of Mark Tobey, Guy Anderson, Louis Bunce, Morris Graves, and Kenneth Callahan, known for the mystical, Asian-inspired language of their painting. Today, artists find the Northwest a place where the pace and cultural climate allow them to create unencumbered by the energy drain of schmoozing with patrons. Our crafts, whether influenced by the early Native-American carvings of the Northwest coastal tribes, Asian traditions, or the contemporary regional idioms emerging from our Arts and Crafts schools, are gaining national attention. And although occasionally one of our artists makes the pages of a national magazine with her cutting-edge work, it's just as easy to spot a menagerie of creatures spawned by a chain-saw sculptor lining any lonely highway. An earnest collector owns a piece by both.

This is the Northwest paradox, and the essence of its style.

In *Northwest Style,* I have attempted to capture that essence by presenting a collection of homes that embody the architecture, style, lifestyle, and spirit of the Northwest. This book is organized into six chapters, each emphasizing an important element of Northwest style. By organizing the book this way, I make a case that while Northwest style is eclectic, informal, and by nature organically driven, our architectural diversity is nothing less than remarkable. Many elements of the chapters overlap. A house designed as a paean to nature, for example, may also have an open floor plan and use native materials, an element of early Regional Modernism. A chic urban loft may express nuances of Japanese design. A house exemplary for its imported materials and avant-garde design may also have a setting that seems like a shrine to the natural elements. And the chapter on artists, cooks, and other creative personalities reveals more about how the spirit of the individual shapes the structure she lives in than its architectural form or function. But while our style is varied, a strong response to the environment and the desire to embellish the natural beauty of the region lies at the heart of almost each design represented in these pages and connects the souls of each dweller.

We begin with the early Modernist classics. Once an isolated little corner of the country, the Northwest borrowed architecture from the rest of the country up until the 1920s. We had our Victorians, colonials, craftsman-style bungalows, and English Tudors, to name a few. Then in the late 1920s and 1930s, some visionary architects and designers began to design in the International style using native materials. The Northwest began to emerge as a unique region of Modernist-style architectural independence. Later established as a formal movement, it became known as Northwest Regionalism, also called early Modernist style. Many still argue about whether Northwest Regionalism, with its inherent conservatism, rates the imprimatur of its own genre, but defenders of the style are passionate about its place in history as a specific vernacular. Regionalism responded to the Northwest's unique challenges in ways that previous architecture did not. It maximized light and views through shapes, sizes, and placement of windows; used deep, overhanging roof lines to protect houses from snow, rain and pine needles; integrated houses with their specific environments; used native and natural materials whenever possible; used open floor plans; and responded to clients' budgets and lifestyles. Regionalism also often incorporated subtle nuances of Japanese style, in landscaping, the use of somber colors, and the simplicity of details.

Detractors, however, consider Regionalism a watered-down derivative of borrowed forms: International, Arts and Crafts, and Prairie styles, to name a few. Some critics consider this style, with its fundamental utilitarianism and its limited ornamentation, to be self-effacing to a fault. As one local, who chose to remain anonymous, explains, "Regionalism is about as seductive as a sensible, midcalf raincoat in a nice shade of beige."

Regionalism made its first gentle imprint in architect A. E. Doyle's simple 1916 cottages, designed with native materials, at Neahkanie beach in Oregon. In 1925, Italian-born architect Pietro Belluschi arrived in Oregon, bringing with him a European sensibility, a Cornell University education, and an open mind. Traveling throughout the region, regarding the simple forms of the old sheds, graceful barns, covered bridges, and humble fish canneries, Belluschi began to define an indigenous look. Along with self-taught designer John Yeon, Belluschi began designing in the International style using native materials and regional forms. By 1935, the Northwest was earning international fame among architectural circles; we had developed a style that was utilitarian, elegant, native, and responsive to the region. Belluschi's homes and buildings stand as the apotheosis of Regional design, distinguished by sensitivity to color, light, shadow, and site, stylish in their simplicity and conceived in a perfect

A full wall of windows accommodates the scale of the trees and the horizontal line of the river below. The lower window panels drop down to the floor, transforming the room from an inside to an outside space.

understanding between the architect and his clients. Belluschi gave the region its first holistic architecture, designs in tune with the visual, social, and spiritual aspects of humanity. The first chapter, "Northwest Regionalism," reflects the Northwest's seminal role in the Modern movement. Five homes, designed by five masters, reveal the purity of form and timeless feel of Regional style, both in its genesis and in its continuation of the tradition. The homes are exciting not only because they are Regional gems but also because their owners share a passion for preserving the style perfected in early Modernism.

Ever since Regionalism first oriented us toward a relationship with nature, we have designed our homes to embrace the elements. Whether building a house on piers over a lake, a house above ground to let natural vegetation flourish below, or a floating home on the river, we are passionate about seeing, feeling, and hearing as much of our environment as we can bring into our lives. The chapter titled "At Home in Nature" focuses on homeowners who made the natural elements the primary focus of their homes.

Today, as the Northwest grows in population and sophistication, designers and architects continue to reinterpret the works of the early Regional masters and those inspired by the Arts and Crafts, International, Modern, and Postmodern movements, with a broader architectural language. We discuss this trend in the chapter called "The New Eclecticism," acknowledging that eclecticism encompasses a lot of elasticity. The homes represented in this chapter reflect the influences of their owners' global travel. These owners bring back treasure—be it a Moroccan wedding chest, or a color, as in Marrakech gold, to be used on the walls. Other homeowners had hefty adjectives such as *rustic* or *rough hewn* in mind when they planned their houses. They sought out architects to create a bold interaction between themselves and the landscape, reflecting both the grit and determination of early settlers and a new, softer Regional romanticism.

As the gateway to the Pacific Rim, the Northwest is strongly influenced by the East, whether in the Zen spirit of nonstriving, the contemplative garden, or a distinct design, such as building a house on a perfect grid. The "East Meets West" chapter illuminates some of the strongest of those influences, melded with a Northwest flavor.

Loft living has become increasingly desirable as urban attractions—theater, music, chic bistros—swell, and the Northwest has become a haven of urban living. The chapter titled "Urban Dwelling"

Untreated, the cabin's board-and-batten cedar siding becomes the silvery shade of the Northwest coast skies. The cabin views Willapa Bay, once teeming with oysters and introduced to Oysterville's founders by Chief Nahcati.

features some of the region's most inspired lofts and condominiums, revealing the owners' passions for books, art, food, and city life.

Finally, as a tribute to both the homes and their dwellers, the chapter called "Artists, Writers, Cooks, and Visionaries" profiles some of our most creative individuals and the personal style that made their homes magical, witty, and warm. These are the people who look at the overgrown, thorny thickets of a landscape gone wild and see the potential for a gorgeous flower garden. They convert barns into houses, houses into cottages, hills into caves.

The homes reflected on these pages are as unique as their dwellers. They were selected for this book not because they are the most palatial, sumptuous, expensive, or painstakingly decorated homes in the Northwest; they're not. Those characteristics are a look, but not typical Northwest style. These homes exude their owners' spirits, even—or especially—in their imperfections. Each house is intensely personal. No homes were propped for photo shoots; we wanted to expose both the beauty and the informality of the Northwest, to show that while our homes carry meaning for us, they are neither precious nor pretentious. Furniture, grouped for conversation instead of shoved against walls, has likely been through a few incarnations. New cabinetry may have been abandoned in favor of a small sailboat; many of us have more money in books than in chairs. For most, our homes are works in progress; we put domestic projects on ice for the day, or for the season, if the snow is perfect powder.

We create environments, not just shelters. Form may follow function, but the human spirit breathes life into the spaces. Nature is our key accessory. We may take our color palette from the bark of a single Douglas fir or build a house around a massive rock. A house on the water will be sited with a nod to sunset, sunrise, and the best of duck symphonies. We design spaces to pull light from the sky. We drag our grills out when the temperature hits fifty-five degrees. Rain dulls the color of the skies. Rain seems endless. Rain soaks our psyches. When the gods are spoon-feeding you rain, you deal with it, sometimes by creating the perfect shelter.

1

northwest regionalism

Early Modern Classics by Five Masters

There is a bench in Portland's Forest Park, a primeval woods thick with old Douglas firs, red alder, Indian plum, plume cedar, Nootka rose, Himalayan blackberry, and Sitka spruce, a woods whose trails wind through the city for fifty miles. The park smells of peat and pine and the fresh-turned earth on the shoes of tireless joggers and wilderness wanderers. On the bench is a small brass plate with a quote from the Northwest's icon of style, Italian-born architect Pietro Belluschi: "A house can never be as beautiful as a tree." ~ In that simple sentence, the late master summarized the soul of Regional style. ~ Some say Regionalism is derivative; others consider it a distinctly Northwest look, but almost everyone agrees that it is organic by nature. Simple and clean, this style bows to the mild climate, abundant rain, elusive sun, and abundance of wood through the use of native materials. It speaks to the dominance of nature (though rules are broken and homes occasionally dominate their landscape) and the importance of light, blurring the boundaries between inside and out through the use of glass. It also contains many elements of Japanese style. Like International style, there

Regionalism embraces the best of modern design in this classic Belluschi design. It is simple, timeless, sophisticated, and makes skillful use of local materials such as wood, brick, and stone.

ABOVE *Rockery is extensive in this garden. A rock wall runs nearly the entire length of the property.* FAR RIGHT *San Juan Island life exists for pleasure. The hammock is strategically placed for the best bird watching, and if eyes should close, listening.*

is a lack of historical embellishment and a great simplicity of form, but similarities end at roof line, building materials, and philosophy. International style announces design; Northwest style announces nature. ~ Pietro Belluschi studied under A. E. Doyle, another Regional master whose simple, unadorned Neahkahnie cottages built in 1916 from native materials are considered by many to be the Northwest style in its nascent form. But it was not until the 1930s that the Pacific Northwest began to earn international fame when Belluschi, along with self-taught designers John Yeon and Van Evera Bailey, set the template for the Northwest tradition by using native materials in the International style. ~ Yeon graced us with the Northwest Regional archetype when he designed the Watzek house in Portland, Oregon, in 1937. A perfect example of Regional style, its composition is so sensitive, the floor plan so harmonious, the features so ingenious, and the form so contemporary, that it serves as an icon to architecture students throughout the region. In Seattle, Paul Hayden Kirk, Paul Thiry, and Roland Terry were a few of the masters who helped to adapt the International style to the Northwest, softening it with the naturalism of native materials. Continuing the tradition was a second generation of architects, among them Walter Gordon, John Storrs, Curtis Finch, William Fletcher, William Farr, Norman Zimmer, and Saul Zaik. ~ This chapter profiles homes designed and maintained in the Northwest Regional tradition. Simple and elegant, with a nod to nature, they remain contemporary classics—designed by Regional masters.

AN EARLY DESIGN BY BELLUSCHI

John and Janet Jay's Portland House

When John and Janet Jay moved to Portland from New York a few years ago, they had no idea they were buying the house Pietro Belluschi designed for himself in 1937; they just liked the "good bones" of the place. Timeless architecture doesn't need to shout; it attracted the Jays with more of a whisper.

The house embodies an eloquent simplicity characteristic of the Northwest master's early career: a design that fits comfortably into the surrounding sloped home site, a U-shaped floor plan close enough to the street to allow for a private garden notched from the terrain in back, a pitched roof with a deep overhang, and the use of native materials. The deep red brick on the exterior, for example, was an inexpensive local earthenware tile. When split into long, thin rectangular bands, it resembled Frank Lloyd Wright's Roman brick.

This is one of several homes the Jays occupy; their others are a renovated barn in Connecticut and a New York loft. They could have chosen any Portland home, but they selected an understated Regional gem with pure and simple lines, high ceilings, bay windows, and an enclosed courtyard of native plantings terraced into the hillside. John Jay is the creative director for Weiden and Kennedy, one of the world's most successful advertising firms, and the people who put the slogan "just do it" into our collective unconscious. Both John and Janet were formerly executives with Bloomingdales in New York. Their exposure to fashion, art, and culture has given them a worldly outlook on style.

The Jays have paid homage to the house's architectural significance by sustaining its character through their use of early Modern decor. Their furnishings are twentieth-century classics, and the couple's creative impulses make the house seem young, fresh, and innovative. The Jays have combined a refined beauty with a contemporary flavor. John combs garage and estate sales and antique stores for much of the furnishings, and many pieces were pulled from their New York home. The art includes Man Ray's drawings of a girlfriend, photos of Coco Chanel and other luminaries by internationally known photographer Horst.

ABOVE *The hillside house makes extensive use of native stones and woods, creating the classic Northwest look introduced by the master of Northwest Modernism, Pietro Belluschi.* FAR LEFT *The dining room cabinet is made of wood and Lucite and was crafted by a German designer. Elegance, class, restraint, and wit define the decor.*

ABOVE *The fifteen squares of photographs, by Portland photographers Richard Kraft and Joe Biel, represent an exploration of the literary themes of Franz Kafka.* LEFT *The painting over the fireplace is of a New York bar scene and was done by a friend of the Jays. With humor, it pays homage to John Jay's parents, who came from China. The painting defuses their fear of Mao Tse-tung's evil empire by rendering the leader a shallow and elite American.* FAR LEFT *A Cyrus Wakefield chest is flanked by two chairs from the 1940s that John Jay found at a garage sale.*

LEFT *The kitchen, updated in granite, stainless steel, and native woods, pays homage to the original design's simplicity.* RIGHT *The bay window extends to a private courtyard garden. The kitchen table, which resembles a Frank Lloyd Wright design, was once a door to an Ohio artist's studio. The studio had caught fire, and the door still bears the elegant, asymmetrical charcoal "graffiti" of fire damage. The chairs are "semi-arm chairs" by designer Gilbert Rohde, manufactured by Herman Miller in the 1930s.* BELOW *The cabinet was built especially for displaying John Jay's extensive collection of globes.*

Marilyn Ridder and Mark von Bergen's Portland House

Architect John Storrs, one of Portland's masters of Regional style, had the perfect clients for one of his first houses designed in the early 1950s: a young couple with cultivated tastes, $25,000 to spend on a small home, and a reverence for the homesite to match his own.

The original owner's son, Mark von Bergen, and his wife, Marilyn Ridder, now hold the title. The hillside house in the trees endures as a classic example of modest Regional style.

Clear cedar, maple, birch, and stone comprise most of the native materials used. The broad roof line follows the open ceiling beyond the house to become an overhanging shelter from rain, snow, and pine needles; this type of roof line is typical of early Modern style. Seven-foot-high interior walls shape spaces, and floor-to-ceiling windows frame more than an acre of southern forest as well as a majestic vista of Mt. Jefferson.

Marilyn, an interior designer, was drawn to the house for its Japanese simplicity and its use of natural materials. The open floor plan and lack of ornamentation that summarize Regional style spoke to her instinct for clarity. Improvements were necessary, however, to bring the house up to date. The kitchen, for example, was transformed from a 1950s nook into a sleek space with stainless-steel countertops and maple cabinets. Although she liked the look and feel of the cork floors—a Storrs signature—they were difficult to maintain and they too easily absorbed the messes made by a toddler. Marilyn replaced them with rich black, gold, and sage green slate, earthy tones that don't attempt to contradict the frequent gray days. She laid the same slate in the bathroom, ran it up the shower walls, and replaced the old bathroom countertop with black granite. Because so much of their family time is spent outdoors, the couple added a large back deck to the house.

The classic lines and simple features of the house have been enhanced by Marilyn's remodel, which balanced contemporary updates with stylistic restraint. The house remains a treasured understatement and a tribute to Northwest Regionalism.

ABOVE *The simple early 1950s cottage is classically Northwest. The cedar siding is painted gray to blend in with the most frequent color scheme of the sky.* RIGHT *The sofa is by Italian designer Vico Magistratti. The painting is by East Coast artist Melinda Stickney Gibson. The color palette reflects the more somber Japanese tones reminiscent of Regionalism. The lamp is an Isamu Noguchi.*

The Great Utopia
TROPICAL BAMBOO
NATURAL

ABOVE *The house is enveloped by woods, and despite rain, the deck serves as a frequent family gathering place. The new deck mirrors the symmetry of the deep overhang, necessary for catching the abundance of pine needles.* RIGHT *The slate floor in the kitchen is an African multi pattern, keeping the home's surfaces in tones of warm bronze, brown, gray, black, and sage green.* FAR RIGHT *The bathroom was remodeled to achieve the simplistic and serene feel of a Japanese bath.*

A CARRIAGE HOUSE'S SECOND ACT

Doug and Selby Key's Portland House and Gardens

ABOVE *Dip and Mack, the family dogs, wait for lunch near their room.* FAR LEFT *The 1910 carriage house, now entirely enveloped by gardens, received a Northwest-style remodel. Fletcher designed windows to let in light and to have garden views from every room.*

When Doug and Selby Key moved to Oregon from the East Coast in the mid-1980s, they left an 1813 Federal-style house. They had torn that house down to the studs, renovating it completely in painstaking detail. The idea of restoring another historical gem seemed daunting, yet while house hunting in Portland, they found themselves revisiting the same house in the southwest part of the city. The Keys were seduced by the 1910 carriage house but decided they would be crazy to buy it. Then they bought it. "I knew we would drive by it forever saying, "We should have bought that house," says Selby. The late Portland architect William Fletcher, a master in the Regional tradition, expanded the house from 900 square feet to 3,000 square feet, with only one proviso: the couple wanted to live with art, a piano, and an Oriental rug and to never yearn for furniture. "We wanted something totally serene, totally contemporary, totally simplified that honored the site." In short, the house had to look good naked. "We went for art over acquisitions," says Selby.

Fletcher created an intimate living area with a twenty-five-foot ceiling and doors that open to the sculpture garden, where Selby's passions, art and gardening, merge. The fireplace now has a stainless-steel surround. A contemporary kitchen sits where coal was once dumped, and beyond that is the den, often claimed by the couple's two Labrador retrievers.

The upstairs master suite is a monochromatic chamber of calm. Television and medical journals (Doug Key is a dermatologist) are taboo. "I want us to spend the last forty-five minutes of the day with the mind, not the personality," says Selby.

After many years here, the Keys have conceded to a few furnishings but have kept them simple. The art, works by internationally known artist Richard Serra and Regional artists including Jay Backstrand and Dale Chihuly, reveals the couple's passion for visual beauty and their cultivated taste. The Keys are such aesthetic purists that they keep one room entirely empty just because they like the way it looks and the energy it lends to the rest of the house. The garden, though, is the soul of the house. When Doug and Selby bought the property, the acre of land was overgrown with weeds. They waited for several years to plant trees so that sun could revitalize the hungry soil while they converted the wild tangles into a garden. Now dozens of species of flowers, outdoor sculpture by Northwest artists such as Lee Kelly, and native evergreens can be seen from every window in the house. Maintaining such pleasing vistas takes time and a great deal of energy. Doug takes the front garden, Selby the back. "We really don't let each other mess with our garden spaces," she says. "We're a little proprietary."

ABOVE *Selby grows several varieties of roses, which do so well in the Northwest that Portland is nicknamed "the rose city."* LEFT *The antique French bread-kneading table holds a vessel by Dale Chihuly, the Seattle artist who revolutionized glassblowing and who has become an icon to Northwest collectors. Like every room downstairs, this room opens to gardens.* RIGHT *Selby's office looks out onto a bed of color and native Northwest plants. The sculpture is by Ronna Neuenschwander.*

OPULENT REGIONAL CLASSIC

A Timeless Walter Gordon Design in Portland

Walter Gordon was one of Portland's venerated second-generation architectural masters. Continuing the ideals of Pietro Belluschi and John Yeon, Gordon shaped much of Portland's best Regional architecture. He was also one of the first architects in the Northwest to blend architecture and art. An urban renewal and environmental activist and a tireless advocate of better design, Gordon slew the encroaching dragons of tract mansions and retropalazzos up until his death in 1997.

Gordon designed this expansive and opulent house in southwest Portland in the late 1960s, when he was in partnership with John Hinchliff, another architect who continued the tradition of Regionalism. Fluid, expressive, and dramatic, while still maintaining the requisite understatement of early Modern design, the house reflects the best of the Regional tradition. Its broad sheltering roof that falls gracefully with the slope of the site, the asymmetrical open floor plan, native woods, large windows, and Asian nuances, particularly in the gardens, render it a classic.

Minutes from downtown Portland, the house represents Regional design, but not typical clients; many of the late architect's clients were quite affluent. The owners bought the house in the late 1980s. They wanted an open floor plan for hosting business and charitable events, a private site with room for tennis courts and extensive gardens, and a luxurious home with a Northwest signature.

Interiors are separated into formal and casual areas with corresponding decor. In the living room, for example, the focus is on the view and, especially in winter, the travertine marble fireplace. Traditional chairs and sofas, upholstered in solid pale neutrals, allow the architecture to make the statement. The heart of the house is the den, paneled in salvaged six-hundred-year-old clear pine. The owners have furnished the house casually and accented it with Native American artifacts.

And while the heart of the house is the den, its soul is the staircase, an exquisite spiral of solid oak gracefully curving from the entry and illuminated by a skylight above.

THIS PAGE *The house is integrated into its extraordinary setting and the Northwest landscape. Regional design is totally livable; the simplicity of forms makes the house timeless. Rocks, roof line, and textures compose an Asian scene.* FAR LEFT *The oak spiral stairwell is as graceful as a line of Japanese calligraphy.*

ABOVE *Unlike the main house, the caretaker's cottage is expressed in saturated color and European eloquence: antiques, artifacts, and art.* LEFT *The living room floor-to-ceiling fireplace is of travertine marble. The windows frame southern vistas.* RIGHT *A Native American–accented sitting room off the master bedroom is the ideal spot for relaxing in front of the fire with a good book.*

Orcas Island Homeowner's Seaside Escape

THIS PAGE *Sunset views of Skull Island. A birdbath draws local species.* FAR LEFT *The family dog runs the dock to the family boat several times a day to check out visitors. The house is enveloped in the back by a stand of fir trees and completely open to the water in the front.*

Orcas Island is one of the Northwest's best escapes for those looking to leave behind the fast-paced, clock-checking rhythms of urban days. A place of tame tempers and no stoplights, Orcas is one of the four largest of 743 islands (there are that many at low tide, and 428 at high tide) that comprise the breathtakingly beautiful San Juan Island chain. Nestled in the rain shadow of the Olympic Mountains, the islands get about half as much rain each year as Portland and Seattle. Visitors, many of whom arrive by ferry, feast on the fresh produce and delectable seafood that has delighted locals for years.

A moss-covered split-rail fence meanders through Douglas fir, cedar, maples, and spruce trees to end at one of the most elegant and welcoming homes on the island: a sky-gray, cedar-shingled rambler trimmed in fir green. With a broad, overhanging roof and a simple façade reminiscent of a Cape Cod classic, the Eastern Shore vernacular has been reinterpreted for a Northwest setting. The roof is made of a low-maintenance copper and slate, and the interiors gleam with native woods, which cover both floors and walls. The site represents the best elements of Northwest nature: the drama of the sea, tiny islands covered in old-growth timber, boats that brush the seascape with colorful sails, and the constant symphony of birds.

The late Portland architect Norman Zimmer designed the house in the late 1980s for a couple who fell in love with Orcas after visiting the island from Portland on their private boat.

Outdoor living is the height of island pleasure. The house is sited to take in sweeping views of Massacre Bay and Scull Island, the latter a tiny mythical-looking plot of tree-covered earth owned by the Bureau of Land Management and inhabited by bald eagles.

To accommodate as much outdoor living as possible, Zimmer designed 5,000 feet of charcoal slate patio to encircle the back of the home. A glass-walled terrace rescues days when winds off the sound are too strong or the days are too cool. Glass walls also surround the "rabbit garden," a plot of land for vegetables and flowers planted for an extended growing season.

The sea-level living area is essentially a large great room, furnished in an eclectic and colorful mix of pieces that define conversation areas. A wall of windows faces the sea, and furnishings are placed for taking in stunning views. Interior details are an intriguing mix of European luxury, Northwest art, and collections such as rabbits, cookbooks, porcelain, and books that fill the rooms. The owner has a striking collection of palm-sized North Coast Indian presentation masks. These intricately carved treasures are so ornamental that she often slips one onto a silk cord to wear around her neck.

Materials, in typical Northwest style, are a comfortable mix of old and new, exotic and regional, elegant and casual. The fireplace surround is of 350-year-old carved French limestone. Native cedar lines floors and walls. A palette of sunny colors and a confident mix of patterns in plaids, florals, and stripes brighten sofas and chairs. European antiques and one-of-a-kind pieces by Northwest craftspeople mix with the owner's own furniture designs—large, receptive sofas and deep, enveloping easy chairs.

The sense of scale is bold, giving the traditional pieces a forceful punch. Even the big books stacked on the rowboat-sized coffee table are grouped to create a sense of balance with the furnishings. "I try to put the largest thing possible in the smallest of spaces," she says. The owner has pulled the look from her own requirements for living: an easy elegance and a relaxed style that's inviting, not imposing.

FAR RIGHT *The master bedroom is painted and furnished in soft watery hues, bringing water imagery indoors. The owner's fondness for rabbits is cleverly revealed in her glass-topped coffee table. The bedframe is covered in a bright Caribbean print fabric.* BELOW *The table was designed by an island artist. The chairs were bought from an old hotel, then taken to an automobile shop for a coat of high-gloss persimmon lacquer.*

ABOVE *The owner's appreciation of the art of Northwest coastal tribes extends to the exterior of the home. The totem is a carving by Glen Tallio, a native of Northwest coast tribe Bella Coola.* LEFT *The flowers are from the garden. The table almost always awaits friends for lunch or dinner. A dining room rug would have limited the use of native wood, one of the owner's favorite materials. Instead, she commissioned Ron Wagner of Portland to stencil a fruit pattern onto the wood floor.* RIGHT *Both intimacy and grandeur are achieved on this slightly sloping site. The hillock off the living room's slate-covered veranda becomes a natural terrace. To the left, a glass-encased "rabbit garden" allows for an extended growing season.*

AT HOME IN NATURE

Celebrating the Elements

The single imperative in the Northwest home is that land comes first. We build our houses around nature, then draw nature back on us worshipfully. We have an insatiable need for the elements and we blur the boundaries between inside and out in as many ways as we can. ~ From the earliest architectural expression of Northwest Regional style, we have oriented our living to embrace nature. We are passionate gardeners, planting gardens that stay in our memories for a lifetime. We work endless hours in spring and summer, digging, weeding, fertilizing, and watering, rewarded by a bowl of bush beans that we scoop from the bowl like pearls or by the luscious fragrance of cut roses. ~ One of the most distinct Northwest lifestyles is the houseboat as habitat. Houseboats range from shanties to swank floating mansions, with dwellers as varied as the dwellings. Professionals, artists, laborers, and people who escape weekend rural digs to work in the city leave land for water at the end of the day. Bobbing on the gentle waves of the region's lakes and rivers, the boaters view the constantly changing river life as performance art. ~ This chapter highlights a few homes whose owners have made access to the elements their guiding passion.

A soft glow of light illuminates the cabin at dawn, where sunrises become an art form. At both dawn and dusk, the folk minimalism and haunting simplicity of the cabin evoke a gothic fairy tale.

Mike and Maya Allsop's Lake Whatcom Contemporary

THIS PAGE *Clear cedar-shingle siding, lake and mountain views, numerous decks, and a setting in a second-growth forest make the Allsop's home quintessentially Northwest.* FAR LEFT *Wicker chairs from Pier One are placed for lake views. The decks are purple heartwood, weathered to a silvery gray. Clematis climbs the arbor.*

It's almost like sleeping in the bow of the ship, all tucked in, the clear water lapping below. Before one of their remodels, the house *did* move like a ship, swaying slowly, keeping pace with the lake's music. "It was exciting but a little unsettling," Maya Allsop says. "We decided the excitement had to go." The house is the only one left that is suspended over Lake Whatcom's glassy surface. Today it could not be built: Washington's environmental restrictions on shoreline building prohibit sharing the lake quite so intimately.

The original blueprint called for the house to be over the water with a bridge access. Pilings, some cemented into the bedrock, some driven, held the wood frame in place. The house was built in 1969, from a design by Bellingham architect Sid Nesbit, and Mike and Maya Allsop have raised a family there. But the house had to grow along with the family. Local architect Dave Ernst helped the couple through a series of four remodeling projects to keep it functional, and above all, to keep the focus on the lake.

The rooms were designed as a paean to the lake setting, with large picture windows placed on three sides of the house. Living and dining areas were sited to catch sunrises over Mt. Baker. The home's natural beauty and elegance are achieved in part by the contrast of several dark and pale woods and by the use of natural materials in the architecture. Pennsylvania bluestone, a slate that changes hues from iridescent green to deep aubergine to granite gray, with the sky's reflections off the lake, is used in the fireplace and to encase the piers below.

The floors and cabinets are made of bullet wood from Guyana, the walls are of clear Ponderosa pine, the decks (upper and lower) are of purple heartwood, also from Guyana. The furniture is deep, comfortable, and receptive, casual enough to drop into after a hike in the nearby foothills of the Cascade Mountains.

For the interior colors, Maya has chosen natural sage greens and earth tones to blur the boundaries between the house and its site. She has selected fabric textures to complement the imperfections of nature. The colors were chosen scientifically: if the hairs from their

ABOVE *One of two kitchen islands, this one was designed to blend with living-area woods and furnishings.* RIGHT *The shower door is made of mahogany. The light and dark woods and the soft curves are intentionally reminiscent of the Allsops' sailboat, perfect for a couple who prefer water to land.* FAR RIGHT *Contrasting woods throughout the house provide a natural sense of style.*

golden retrievers disappeared into it, the fabric was in the running. With two big dogs, frequent houseguests, and numerous trips to and from the lake, camouflage was a design priority.

The couple can't imagine ever leaving the lake, claiming they would miss the natural theatrics too much. Beaver spottings are a daily event, eagles sweep by frequently, and mother geese, protecting their goslings, honk at ear-piercing decibels.

The Allsops love to entertain, both for friends and as a part of the international business they have developed over several decades. The couple turn the breaking of bread into a ceremony, and dinner parties, often for crowds of ten, are frequent events. The mahogany dining table, an Arthur Brett design from Harrod's, is laid with Waterford crystal. Maya recalls a dinner for a group of Pacific Rim clients who were visiting the Northwest for the first time, enjoying Pacific salmon and other regional foods at her table. "We were all admiring the sunset when a deer leaped in front of us, almost close enough to touch. One guest looked at me in disbelief. 'How did you do that?' he asked. I told him I pushed the deer button."

ABOVE *The dogs, often wet from a swim, are trained to enter from the lake level below. They "dry off" in the utility room.* LEFT *Guests who arrive by boat enter at lake level. The house has been anchored to the bedrock, ensuring earthquake protection.* FAR LEFT *Decks provide outdoor living for about forty days of the year.*

Buzz and Pam Gorder's Willamette River Houseboat

This houseboat has got to be the diva of river dwellings, a sumptuous, swanky, brilliant floating home on the banks of the Willamette River in Portland. With its curved, delineated, cloverleaf sides and double-domed roof, it's rather like a chrome-dipped Le Corbusier on a liquid lot. Buzz and Pam Gorder's 2,800-square-foot houseboat offers them the perfect lifestyle: no grass to mow, no pool to clean, and a view to rival anybody's anywhere. The reflection of the setting sun on Portland's downtown turns the house a brilliant gold. Tugboats, barges, and sailboats, their colorful sails snapping in the wind, form part of the riverscape. Then there's the wildlife. "Where else do you get to live with eagles as eye-level neighbors?" asks Pam.

Buzz Gorder designed the houseboat, drawing on his years of river life and ideas he's gathered traveling as a trade-show exhibit designer and manufacturer. The roof barrels, for example, are vaults from barn silos he discovered while driving through Illinois farmland.

The shiny anodized metal is continued in the interiors of the houseboat in horizontal or vertical slats. Outside, the metal reflects the hues of the river and sky. Inside, the splash of colors makes the interiors vibrant, even on winter's grayest days.

LEFT *Exterior columns of spiraling metal sheeting enhance the houseboat's fluid design. One of the couple's vintage motorboats zips them to river gatherings and harborside restaurants in style. The floating home's showy features slow passersby down to a lazy drift. Most of the river's houseboats are clad in wood, and model traditional cabins.* RIGHT *Large corrugated-aluminum planter boxes mirror the houseboat's design and provide a deck garden over the water. The table is a hand-painted geometric design on wood with a thick coat of clear sealer.*

LEFT *Color squeezes warmth into the spaces and keeps the whole place moving. Most surfaces are high gloss, reflecting the water below and the cityscape across the river.* BELOW *Bold shots of saturated color reveal the Gorders' creative spirit and help them forget that winter days can be long and dark. The glare is absorbed in part by the strong interior wall colors.*

RIGHT *The bath was designed partly to reflect the colors of the river and sky. Raising the tiled tub and keeping windows high allows for privacy.* FAR RIGHT *The bedroom was sited for privacy but still allows for more distant river views. A circular skylight above the bed provides for fabulous evening views.*

Jeffrey Biben and Peggy Bosley's Vacation Home

This Willamette Valley family retreat was conceived over a glass of fine Australian red wine. Jeffrey Biben's parents, who reside Down Under, were lamenting the difficulties of wending their way up and down the West Coast of the United States every summer, trying to fit every family member into their brief visit. They joked about buying a transportable cabin and dropping it in one spot in the States so that the family could visit *them* for a change.

Jeffrey and his wife, Peggy Bosley, both architects in Claremont, California, began planning a summer camp to serve as a family gathering place. The five-acre site with views of the Willamette River near Eugene was ideal for a communal vacation. These city dwellers would share the space with deer and birds and relax among the huge old black oaks, wild lilies, irises, and native blackberries in some of the most beautiful wilderness in the Willamette Valley.

The design program for the cabin was simple: open and uncluttered living spaces with small eating and sleeping areas, a detached space for guests, and a carport.

The design shows a respect for the quiet but rugged natural beauty of the site. Built up off the ground in the post-and-beam style to minimize disruption to the existing topography, the cabin allows natural vegetation to thrive under and around it. Reminiscent of Native-American longhouses, the only structures to touch the ground are the fireplace and a curved shower with a glass ceiling and small windows placed for viewing deer. Inside, the space is rustic and peaceful, with vaulted ceilings maximizing volume and views of the river and wild vegetation.

The use of low-maintenance materials, such as corrugated galvanized metal siding for the guest house, Douglas fir plywood for the floors, ceilings, and cabinets, and sheet metal for the kitchen countertops, kept cost under control without sacrificing good looks. Along with being cost-conscious, the owners also intentionally chose humble materials to keep the focus of the vacation retreat on the natural beauty of the site.

ABOVE *The family summer camp is comfortably rustic and, at night, voluptuously dramatic. Built of heavy timbers with a steeped, pitched metal roof to prevent fire and shed rain, and with deep overhanging eaves to provide shade, its rustic simplicity evokes the old sheds and covered bridges on Oregon's rural roads.* FAR LEFT *Peggy and Jeffrey designed the simple Mission-style furniture as well as the rusticated fireplace surround, made of concrete block. The blankets are the Northwest's own Pendleton.*

ABOVE *The "outdoor" shower gives the feeling of a summer camp for grownups.* RIGHT *The bathroom shower and floor is of unglazed ceramic tile. Most of the materials for the cabin were bought from local and inexpensive sources to keep costs under control.* FAR RIGHT *The cabinets were crafted from Douglas fir marine-grade plywood. The floors were laid in 1 x 4 pine plywood.*

ABOVE *The riverside hamlet is sheltered by old oaks and suffused with some of the Northwest's wettest sunlight.*
RIGHT *Natural vegetation thrives underneath the cabin. The cabin recalls images of early Native American longhouses.*
LEFT *A simple maple dining table is situated for a view of the black oaks. An aboriginal bark painting hangs on the wall above.*

Sydney and Nyel Stevens's Folk Cabin in Oysterville

This cabin is a miniature house with a maximum story; a place where five rivers and a million memories meet. A few feet beyond a moss-encrusted gate, an evocative shape rises like a gothic dollhouse from J. R. R. Tolkien's Middle Earth, so intimate with its environment that it becomes a private world.

It was not Sydney Stevens's intent to build a Hobbit house in Oysterville, the northernmost point on the Long Beach Peninsula; her life just unfolded that way. As a girl growing up in the Bay Area, Sydney spent her summers in Oysterville, the community founded by her great-grandfather, Robert Espy. Espy and his business partner, I. A. Clark, both Pennsylvanians, were timber cruisers who visited the peninsula in 1854. Guided in canoes by Chief Nahcati to beds of oysters, where they stood knee-deep, the men began trading the delicate, succulent bivalves. Soon an industry was born, and oyster schooners and tales of the sea became a part of the local fabric.

THIS PAGE *Leaded glass windows in the cabin's tiny entry reflect the dappled light of sunset.* FAR RIGHT *Seeing the cabin illuminated at night, one visitor remarked, "It looks like it has been there forever." Bay waters are laced with sand verbena, sea rocket, beach pea, and lupine. Red-tailed hawks soar above the horizon.*

Sydney became established as a schoolteacher in San Francisco, but she continued to vacation on the Long Beach Peninsula. In the late 1970s, she bought twelve acres of Oysterville bayside property, thick with arrow grass, wild strawberry, lupine, and pickleweed. Almost serendipitously, she was offered a teaching job at a Long Beach grammar school, which she accepted. Noel Thomas, a local watercolorist and craftsman, designed the house. Noel and Sydney were old friends; though Noel is not an architect, his first sketches captured what she had envisioned. Another local, German-born craftsman Ossie Steiner, built the house from Noel's drawings.

The 900-square-foot cottage is a departure from the quaint romantic vernacular of Oysterville's old Victorian houses, most of which are made of California redwood, reused from the ballasts of ships that arrived for trade. With its cedar board-and-batten siding, simple A-frame, open floor plan, and rustic charm, it is more reminiscent of the fish canneries, covered bridges, boathouses, and old barns of the region.

Seven large windows framing the bay are generously fitted with window seats for bayside views; the floor is a rich red fir. The wood-

watch cat
MATCHES

stove wall is laid in bricks that Sydney salvaged from an old boathouse, spending a summer scraping off their old mortar. Blue-stained pine, sometimes called blue and buggy wood, panels the walls, the rough side exposed. "Much to Ossie's dismay," says Sydney of the craftsman/builder who was so attentive to perfection and smooth surfaces that he pleaded with Sydney to turn the wood over. Exposing the texture is in keeping with the cabin's rough-hewn style, and it also mirrors the variegated textures found on the sandy beaches beyond.

The decor is simple and humble. Sydney and her husband, Nyel, who runs the Book Vendor, their bookstore in Long Beach, didn't want any furnishings to detract from the natural setting. Drawings and paintings by her children, oak antiques she traded for baby-sitting and hotel watching in off-seasons, record albums, and enough books to escape into for years provide enough comforts for any creature.

ABOVE *Old Adirondack chairs and a worn rope rail are all that the decking needs.* LEFT *Windows frame Willapa Bay and look out onto federally protected Long Island, where an old-growth forest thrives.* FAR LEFT *The kitchen's open shelves hold old canning jars of legumes and grains. A house blessing, bestowing health and happiness, was carved by the builder into the first post of the stairwell.*

Linda and Wilbur Kukes's Bellingham House

Early on the lake, when it is very quiet and still, the Kukeses can hear the honking of geese, which are so close that there is a perceptible rush of air as they pass over and form a silvery wishbone in the stormy sky above the Olympic Mountains.

Life here on Lake Whatcom, ten miles in from Bellingham Bay in northwest Washington, is like camp for grownups. Eagles, deer, beavers, and geese are common sights. The natural beauty evokes a perpetual awe, with only occasional tremors in the calm. There are sunsets that leave lake dwellers speechless and cougar sightings that prompt them to lock up their pets for the night.

Wilbur and Linda Kukes's Arts and Crafts lodge-style bungalow was designed as an idyllic home for an idyllic setting. The site was once an old family camp, and one of the original cottages, refurbished as a guest house, accommodates family and friends who come for luxurious escapes into nature.

The house had to fit in well with two environments, forest and lake. It would have been easy to overdevelop the site, given the eight hundred feet of lake frontage and five acres of land. The architect, David Hall of Mt.Vernon, Washington, was sensitive to the site and designed the house to live large and look small. From the curved driveway entrance, through the silvery shafts of light filtering through the old pines and firs, the red cedar–shingled house sits quietly like a glorious summer lodge awaiting a cast of elegant guests.

The covered entry evokes bungalow and craftsman-style features such as wide eaves and broad roof overhangs to reduce the scale of the house and to impart a rustic, Japanese-style grace. Extensive glazing, dozens of skylights, and more contemporary materials, such as tile and aggregate floors and granite countertops, juxtapose the rustic craftsman features with a contemporary touch.

Inside, the large great room is defined by rough-hewn beams and doubled columns to create intimate spaces. Bay windows overlook the lake from nearly every room in the house. A large outdoor room, accessed from the garage, kitchen, or the great room, is equipped with

ABOVE *The house sits on Georgia Point, a natural sandstone bank thick with native salal.* FAR RIGHT *A built-in redwood bench flanks pre-cast concrete forms, which lay a simple path to the lake below. The landscape architect filled the hollows with low woodland plants. The sculptural stone mounds provide a contrast in form and function with the aggregate and brick grid of the terrace.*

RIGHT *An acrylic by Portland artist C.W. Potzz gives wit to the entry.* BELOW *The oversized chaise and ottoman are covered in smoky sage chenille. They make a perfect place to read or watch the sun set.* LEFT *Terra-cotta sconces enhance ambient light. Wilbur, a surgeon, was the perfect person to assemble the hanging spheres over the dining table. They are made of paper-thin curved sections of balsa wood.*

a brick fireplace, large grill, informal dining table, and comfortable chairs for reading or daydreaming. Two glass-front garage doors in the outdoor room open to the lake with an easy pull, a nearly irresistible temptation, regardless of the weather. Often storms over the lake make for the best in dining atmosphere.

Furnishings are so tactile that the cat and dog spend their days trading textures—an hour or two on the chaise, a nap on the sofa, wrapping up the day on a Tibetan tiger-stripe rug. The coffee table is crafted of buffalo hide and wicker. Linda chose a chenille fabric for the sofas and chairs that blends the warm, reddish tone of the walls with the tawny tones of the beach grass below. Both Linda and Wilbur have collected art and crafts for over twenty years. Wilbur leans toward primitive and outsider art such as the works of Walter Anderson and Moses T. Linda acquires the works of Northwest artists. The whole look of the house is sophisticated with a rustic feel, a bungalow reinterpreted for owners who live casually and comfortably but with great style.

The walls are painted in tones of sage, cedar, brick, and sea grass, a sampler of the shoreline's range of hues. "The site calls for colors found in the natural setting, and colors that absorb the changes in weather," says Linda, who plants seven hundred red geraniums each summer, a startling urgency of color that she's come to depend on. Some find the number obsessive. She agrees. "Summer is short, color is quick, you've got to squeeze what you can from the season."

Whatever the season, the house, interiors, and setting make for one of the Northwest's most splendid homes. "This house is about the lake, about being seduced by the setting, about being aware of nature. It's always changing out there," says Wilbur.

RIGHT *The fireplace is constructed in a Cape Cod pattern with niches for Japanese, Native American, and local crafts. The bricks were salvaged from a local school yard. The oil painting is by the late Northwest master Carl Morris.*

ABOVE *The red cedar shingles are carried through to the entry, which gathers light from the side windows and above from the skylights. The floor is exposed aggregate, a color repeated in the granite spheres. A painting by Northwest artist John Stahl and pillows by a Skagit county weaver give one side of the room a splash of color. The other side remains monochromatic with raku vessels by local artist Eugene Lewis.*

RIGHT *The walls are painted a baked-brick shade. An oil painting by Northwest artist Drake Deknatel hangs above an old library table Wilbur found in a Montana barn. A collection of vessels by Northwest craftsmen Don Sprague, Pat Horsley, Wally Schwab, and Ruri share space with seventeenth-century Japanese teapots.*

design

ABOVE *The terraces down to the lake are grids of old brick sets filled with smoothly tamped small-stone gravel.* LEFT *The gardens unite nature and architecture in the Japanese style. Nationally known landscape architect Richard Haag, who spent a year studying in Kyoto, Japan, incorporated the mountain element of Japanese gardens into the Kukeses' landscape with these piles of smooth local stones.* FAR LEFT *The indoor/outdoor room serves as the spot for supper most evenings, rain or shine. The rug is a sea-grass sisal woven in London. The room is filled with folk art, native tribal baskets, and the aromas of fresh-grilled Northwest foods.*

The New Eclecticism

Emerging Styles

It's been more than half a century since the Northwest began earning national fame as the mainstream of Regionalism, and times are changing. Humble designs and form-follows-function floor plans worked then and they do now, but today there is more to Northwest style than mollifying the gray skies. ~ We can attribute at least some of the change to the fact that our borders aren't holding. The growth of high-technology industries such as Microsoft and Intel, combined with our spreading national reputation for livability, has opened the Northwest to transplants, people who are kicking our provincialism in the shins and changing the way we look. ~ We are seeing more of a range in design, from the flat-roofed International-style contemporary to the sculptural forms of Italianate villas to postmodern cubes to a revival of the simple folk house, reminiscent of the old sheds, covered bridges, and barns that still grace many rural settings. A loosening of formal strictures has given way to architecture that is more intuitive, sensual, and rebellious and that is not only subordinate to but continuous with the environment. Naked houses—those with exposed trusses, joists, and concrete footings—are subverting

Perched atop a rock outcropping, and in an unending dance with nature, the Barnes's house overlooks the Strait of Georgia, to the mainland of British Columbia, and views the rugged shoreline of Vancouver Island to the Northwest.

ABOVE *Apollo is placed strategically on the veranda to summon the sun. Many of the estancias featured marble statuary both inside the homes and in the courtyards and grounds.* FAR RIGHT *The house's construction materials are made explicit beginning with the entry ramp and foyer: exposed framing, naked paneling, floor joists cut at random lengths, the industrial flash of nuts and bolts.*

classical traditions and speaking to a broader design inquiry. ❧ Materials also possess a new energy. Corrugated metal is used on roofs and exteriors. Wood is still the dominant material in homes, but whereas Regional siding used to be almost exclusively of native woods, now real and synthetic stuccos are used alone or with wood on many contemporary homes. Concrete and stone floors are replacing traditional oak and maple. Brushed, stainless-steel, and slate accents in kitchens and baths are taking the place of vinyl and tile. Indigenous woods—cedar, pine, spruce, and alder—are complemented by aged salvaged woods and more exotic imports such as Honduran mahogany. ❧ One of the most aesthetic benefits of emerging Regional style is the unity of art and architecture. Old architectural details provide beautiful, whimsical, and sometimes witty accents to contemporary homes. Architects and designers are using local craftspeople and artists to create unique details from lighting to fireplaces to furnishings to textured walls and hand-carved doors. Color, once subdued and somber, is breaking out into full-value splashes. ❧ Peter Miller, who for over twenty-five years has owned a Seattle bookstore devoted to books on architecture and interiors, says that Regional style is becoming more assertive, colorful, whimsical, erotic, intuitive, and sensual. "But not overtly sensual. It's too cold here for that. We're still a black-and-white-movie kind of sensual." Adding that respect for the environment is still the Northwest signature, Miller wryly points out that a few people, and in particular those building tract mansions, "consider their homes ecological as long as they don't lose heat." ❧ The homes represented in this chapter offer a look at the emerging style: they are eclectic, intuitive, colorful, rebellious, and sensuous, but through their settings, architecture, or attitude, all are unmistakably Northwestern.

Karol Niemi and Dennis Batke's Portland House

TOP *A view from below the house with gazebo and gardens.* ABOVE *Mediterranean elements begin at the front entry, designed like a European courtyard.* FAR LEFT *Eclectic art and classical architecture are the influence and inspiration of the Niemi Batke home. Each object carries the nobility of being handpicked, making it inescapably dramatic. Black and white, favorite neutrals, are evident in the marble stripes of the tile floor.*

All the colors of Vienna—cinnamon, blood orange, pale gold, ink green—kept running through their dreams every night. Neither one said anything to the other, at least not right away. Then one evening, sitting in a chic Viennese coffeehouse, they were inspired to design their dream home. Over house jug wine and Greek olives, they sketched. Call it marital telepathy, that sharing of one brain that occurs after twenty-five years of togetherness, but they produced identical blueprints on their cocktail napkins. Then they returned home to start building their dream.

Though both Karol Niemi and Dennis Batke were born and raised in Oregon, their house is delightfully un-native. It strongly reflects emerging trends brought back from international travel: strong colors, European design features such as palazzos, colored ceramic tile, important international art, and a departure from native woods and stone. Through the use of double soffits, bold color, and three-dimensional design, the feeling is sculptural, dramatic. The roof line is Moroccan, its color Japanese tile green. The entry is tiled and walled in the style of a European courtyard. One of Portland's most sophisticated contemporary designs, the house looks like a villa in Portofino. The home's four levels are filled with elegant materials, contemporary art, exquisite and rare antiques, and early romantic European design images, all a melding of influences from the couple's annual travels. The floors are inlaid with exotic woods, carpeted in geometrics, or laid in elegant rectangles of black-and-white tile. The walls are energized with shots of saturated color: nasturtium, gold, orange juice, warm pewter, and firecracker red.

The fifty-foot-wide hillside lot in northwest Portland dictated that they build up, not out. The street-level entry floats up to the thirty-foot-high ceiling, and becomes the focal point, the center of the rectangle that forms the spine of the house and divides the symmetry. Mt. Hood, Oregon's tallest peak, is framed by the dining room's double-glass doors. Dennis calls the placement "Our homage to Hood."

ABOVE *The house sits on a fifty-foot-wide hillside that takes in dazzling views of four mountains. It is a narrow house, the interiors manipulated in the European style to feel spacious.* ABOVE RIGHT *The house's three-dimensional sculptural elegance and bold color scheme can be viewed from the upper level. Stair risers are set in bands of black-and-white recycled tile the size of piano keys.* LEFT *The east-portal pattern repeats in the entry (west) portal. The deck chairs are junk-shop finds. The trim paint is a shade Karol mixed called arctic white.*

Because they went vertical with the design, Dennis and Karol tossed out any idea of a formal living area, opting instead for several conversation niches, each a result of inspired design. Some niches invite solitude. The library, for example, is the size of a luxury car, microdesigned so that the architectural details are worthy of the hundreds of books the shelves hold. Its floor has an exquisite herringbone design of three inlaid woods: ash, wenge, and padauk. The Honduran mahogany cabinets are dyed a deep red lacquer, revealing the translucence of the wood's grain, a fine example of using wood to create a strong sense of sophistication.

Other rooms draw in people with a conversation pieces, whether it's a nineteenth-century Chinese altarpiece, an exquisite Moroccan wedding chest, or a chair Karol found at a junk sale for $10 and made voluptuous with Fortuney fabric.

The house reflects a sense of place, a love of Northwest art, and the growing influences of other cultures. "We work very hard," Karol says of her thriving interior-design business and her husband's architecture practice, "and then we make airline reservations."

RIGHT *The house was built as a "homage to Hood," Oregon's tallest mountain. An oil painting by Mexican artist Javaier Fernandez hangs above a sofa that Karol recreated from a 1930s-era found frame.*

ABOVE *The chair adjacent to the sofa is a junk-shop find. The chair was originally in aubergine mohair; then Karol reupholstered it in an English petit-point fabric. The frame was refinished in gold, lapis, and malachite colors. The couple found the Moroccan plates in Fez.* RIGHT *A sliver of the couple's extensive European glass collection sits on the fireplace mantel and includes several pieces by Lino Tagliapietra. The 1940s-era club chairs are recovered in Clarence House fabrics. The coffee table is by Italian designer Frattini.*

Bill Thurston's Medina Contemporary

Bill Thurston, owner of one of the most avant-garde small hotel and athletic facilities in the country, the Bellevue Club Hotel, made his Medina-area home the model for the club's design. "When people walk into this house they feel something intriguing, something of themselves," he says. "I wanted visitors to the club, whether it's Nelson Mandela or the queen of England, to experience the same thing."

The home sits in a quiet neighborhood resplendent with small architectural gems. The surrounding board-and-batten and shingle-sided cottages were once weekend escapes for city dwellers from nearby Seattle. The former owner was a home and garden writer for *Sunset* magazine. Though her house was razed, the gardens were protected and drove the design of Bill's house.

Architect Betty Blount designed a contemporary house with a courtyard orientation and a sophisticated integration of architecture and art. Both exterior and interior lines have strong horizontal and vertical forms through the use of windows, changes in floor and ceiling planes, and roof lines. The forms create a tight geometric precision that makes the use of handcrafted details and artistic embellishments stand out in strong relief. The result is a stunning and stylish contemporary that celebrates the works of local craftspeople and looks like a European villa with a Northwest garden setting.

Living spaces are defined by changes in floor and ceiling planes, partial walls, and private garden courtyards, which open to all the main living spaces. Blount designed the living room ceiling to appear to float. Lower in the middle and raised on the sides, it offers the drama of a high ceiling but confers an intimacy inspired by the private courtyards.

One of the architect's peeves is a corridor that ends in a blank wall. "All these long spaces with no sense of intriguing places one could go," she says. She designed each connecting space to end in a work of art. Artists Judy Mars and Jacques Moitoret painted several doors as canvases, rendering them as abstract elements and disguising their functions. Instead of a hall ending in a plain door to the wine cellar, it's resolved in a pleasant surprise, a colorful abstract image. Interior

ABOVE *The exterior of the house features strong horizontal and vertical lines, geometric shapes, and nuances of International design.* LEFT *The house was built around an existing cork tree.* FAR LEFT *A reading room incorporates contemporary European furniture, designer fabrics, and Northwest art. The curtain fabric was designed by Jack Lenor Larsen, the desk chair is a Dakota Jackson out of New York, and the paintings are by Northwest artist Mark Rediske.*

doors are treated with warm, muted colors. Artists Gerry Newcomb and Ann Gardner designed glass works that actually became portions of plaster walls. Niche elements, heavily textured in color-true plaster, went into the design with specific works of art in mind. Both Bill and the architect were wary of just plugging in to the general marketplace to find art when the project was complete. "A piece of art has a home, rather than hanging on a flat wall," says Bill. "It's as important as a piece of furniture; it's a part of the architecture."

Guided by the architect, Bill tapped into the Northwest contemporary art movement and commissioned local sources as an integral part of the design, from designing furnishings and lighting to texturing walls in colored matte plaster to achieve a handcrafted look. He has amassed an extensive collection of glass and clay works that require a unique method of display. To achieve this, the casework in beechwood, glass, and plaster, designed by craftspeople, is integrated throughout the house. The house is essentially tactile, accomplished in part by the art but also by the use of materials: matte limestone and maple floors, greenstone and marble in the baths, rough-textured textiles mixed with rich chenille and silk fabrics. Turkish, Tibetan, Peruvian, and Asian rugs provide color and texture, ethnic artifacts lend intrigue, and the courtyard views and regional touches pin it to the Northwest.

FAR RIGHT *Two living areas, each with courtyard views, accommodate large crowds for entertaining. The shellacked paper pig sculptures by Rand Smith are from an Arizona gallery. The oil painting is by regional artist Darren Waterson. Most of the furnishings come from Milan or Paris. A Van Campden Turkish carpet and a custom carpet by Joan Wiseman define spaces.* RIGHT *Art and architecture make good bedfellows. The wall niche was designed specifically for New York artist Ming Fay's mixed-media pear.*

ABOVE *The three-quarter-acre site was already planted with mature gardens.* LEFT *Local artists made the kitchen table, chairs, and light fixtures.* RIGHT *Overhead lighting was concealed in the planes of the ceiling. San Francisco artist Pam Morris designed the chandelier. The handcrafted dining table is made of maximum density fiber, a pressed-paper product often used in paint-grade cabinetry, and was inlaid with bronze by Seattle artist Mark Fessler.*

RIGHT *The master bath incorporates marble, stone, and glass.* FAR RIGHT *A guest bedroom reflects the owner's love of folk and ethnic works—and his travels. The bedcover is from India, the bed frame by Seattle metal fabricators 47 Productions. The ceramic shade of the bedside lamp was hand-painted by an East Coast artist. The mix of primitive textiles and contemporary fabrics gives the room artistry in pattern and color with a fresh spontaneity of finish.*

Elinor and John Paulk's Seabeck House

The property had already captured their hearts; now they just had to move the rest of themselves from Illinois. For years, Elinor and John Paulk tent-camped at the site where their home now sits, breathing the fresh scent of cedars and huckleberries and listening to the muscular music of naval ships from a waterfront bluff, two hundred feet above Puget Sound. The site faces the sixty-mile-long saltwater body known as the Hood Canal near Bremerton, Washington, and takes in views of the Olympic Mountains.

The Paulks would catch oysters, crabs, and clams for dinner, cooking them over a campfire. They still do, only now summer supper is served on the deck, and a group of friends often bring dishes to complement the fresh catch.

The couple was ready to retire but wanted to keep in contact with the Bremerton naval community, where John had been a commander before he joined Ferma Labs as an administrator. They had seen Bainbridge Island architect James Cutler's work and liked its natural beauty and informality. "We called his office and they said he was busy for two years," John says. "I said, 'That's great. We won't need him until then.'"

The Paulks had few requirements. "I wanted a workshop," says John. "I wanted a good kitchen—nothing too fancy," says Elinor, who likes the look of the kitchen's unpolished granite counters.

The result is the consummate Northwest design—unplugged. James Cutler's design is in turn whimsical and serious, ordered and serendipitous, practical and profligate, and elegant and raw, deferring to the logic of the landscape and unself-conscious of its beauty and its utility. It is a naked house, its skeletal forms left exposed instead of sheathed in Sheetrock.

The construction was designed to create the minimum amount of disturbance to the wooded site, including a space where the roof and rafters were notched to save a tree. In all only three trees were felled to build the house.

Rising to fourteen feet off the forest floor, the house looks planted in a forest hollow. The entry is accessed by a 117-foot-long ramp that

ABOVE *The house is anchored to the ground at its south end, then rises fifteen feet high off the forest floor at the north end, so that the Hood Canal can be viewed from the first floor. Thin metal cables are strung beneath the cedar handrails, offering only a slight barrier to the forest.* FAR LEFT *The beauty and utility of the house are revealed through the use of natural materials. Views of trees are available in every room except the laundry.*

pierces the house, shooting out the back to end at a belvedere, a solitary platform that dramatically hovers over the edge of a bluff. By the time one reaches the house, the fragrant and fecund beauty of the forest has been experienced, just as the architect intended.

Much of Northwest architecture is rustic and rough-hewn, though finished to perfection. The result is often an abstract concept of beauty, carried through in traditional forms. But this cedar house has a hand-built look. Its beauty is immediate, literal. Inside, ceilings are pulled back to reveal construction materials, and the concrete footings are uneven and look as if they've been wrenched from the earth's womb. Floor joists are cut at random lengths, and some of the ceiling's paneling stops short of the walls, where joists can be viewed. There is an industrial elegance to the materials and their placement. Sheet metal is screwed into place as wall panels; metal connectors and large nuts and bolts become ornamentation. Beams punch through the foyer's interior walls of bleached knotty pine. Wood hinges are exposed; only one of the characteristics of the house that playfully coaxes the eye into deconstructing, then reassembling, it. One of the most interesting idiosyncrasies is the seemingly random toss of the cross-braced posts under the house. There is method to the madness, the Paulks explain. In one sense, the ad hoc placement of the trusses reflects nature's random patterns. The other explanation the Paulks offer is that the architect, who was raised in eastern Pennsylvania, was intrigued by the artful forms of Pennsylvania coal-mining tipples and replicated them in the design.

ABOVE LEFT *The deck pierces the house and ends in back at the belvedere, a place for enjoying dazzling mountain and water vistas.* ABOVE *The concrete footings are a part of the architecture's exposed, raw beauty.* RIGHT *The 117-foot-long entry ramp, flanked by wild rhododendrons, passes through the house and ends at the belvedere, two hundred feet above the cliff. John Paulk laid all the decking on the house.*

LEFT *The framing in the foyer is exposed. The knotty pine walls, common in the Northwest, have been treated with a transparent white stain, rendering them more sophisticated.* FAR LEFT *Most of the dining-area cabinets are built-ins, to simplify the interiors.*

A NORTHWEST ESTANCIA

Sandy and Mike Manion's Columbia Gorge House

This house was inspired by the *estancias*—the splendid rural estates of Argentina—and reinterpreted through a romantic Northwest spirit. The stunning contemporary sits high overlooking the Columbia Gorge on forty acres of woods in Corbett, Oregon—totally unlike the old wood ramblers, historical gems, and craftsman-style bungalows that typify gorge architecture. And though it was built in 1998, it looks as if it's been there forever, which pleases the Manions, who wanted the house to have a centuries-old feeling. "People ask us how long the restoration has gone on," says Sandy Manion, who with her husband, Mike, designed and built the house, which they named Villa Mandala. "It's the highest form of compliment."

The Manions were strongly influenced by the Argentine country style of the *estancias,* which first emerged in the sixteenth century and represented a hybrid of architecture from a range of regions: Spain, England, France, Scotland, and Italy. These voluptuous estates, while devoted primarily to cattle ranching, manifest such independence of spirit and opulence in design that they stand today as a symbol of rugged romanticism.

The uniqueness of this house begins with its virtually colorless exterior. It's a shade similar to the Roman Cement patented in 1796. Leaving the cement stucco exterior plain was one way in which the couple paid tribute to the site. The house doesn't compete with its surroundings; but then little could. The Manions live with coyotes, eagles, and other birds in rural serenity. Lofty basalt cliffs, pure waterfalls, and rock formations cut by the country's second longest river make for intoxicating views. Quick creeks tumble through silvery gray side canyons to reach the Columbia. And all of this is in their back yard. The couple replicated the rustic details of the *estancias* by using a wide range of materials, including recycled rough-hewn beams and salvaged doors from old churches and homes. Tumbled limestone gives some of the floors a European formality; others are laid in beautiful burnished salvaged cherry. The new woods, such as those Mike used for his clear-finished poplar kitchen cabinets, are a handsome

ABOVE *The house is a melding of European architectural styles and Northwest materials, set on a cliff above the Columbia Gorge.* LEFT *Airy verandas were common to the* estancias. *This one, with its rough-hewn columns, was designed by Portland landscape architect Wallace K. Huntington.*

counterpoint to the old. Mike is a woodcrafter; his upscale cabinetry, furniture, and copies of expensive designer pieces can be found in some of the region's most beautiful homes.

Villa Mandala is flooded with color. Many of the *estancias* were washed with hues achieved from mixing such substances as cow's blood with lime wash, and Sandy (though she eschewed cow's blood) went to a good deal of trouble herself to find the perfect shade. Watermelon, curry, pistachio, hazelnut, lime, persimmon, butter: the delicious saturated colors bring the Northwest art and interior details strongly into focus.

The decor is relaxed, eclectic, creative, and a work in progress—just like the Manions. An old wrought-iron gate is turned on its side as a mantel detail; decorative cherubs' heads and Victorian stone garden doves appear spontaneously all over the house. In the powder room, Sandy tossed a piece of gold gift-wrap netting made locally around the window, giving it an informal elegance in keeping with *estancia* decor.

ABOVE *Mike Manion replicated Villa Mandala's oversized entry doors by using a photograph of a pair of French Antique doors.* RIGHT *A view of the Columbia Gorge. Though fog and rain are common elements in the gorge, clear days offer stunning views of nature.* FAR RIGHT *The kitchen floor is of French limestone. Mike made the kitchen cabinets in poplar, a wood that typically receives a coat of paint. Sandy liked the dramatic grain, however, and finished the wood in a clear sealer.*

ABOVE *The colors in Scott Sonniksen's painting are enhanced by the Venetian glass vases and the mercury glass balls.* LEFT *Yards of fabric work as room dividers, a trio of tiger-stripe rugs leads to the living area, and color warms up every room.* FAR LEFT *A painting by Portland artist Scott Sonniksen hangs on the back wall of the living room.*

Fran and Dave Barnes's Vancouver Island House

ABOVE *A browlike canopy extends out over the structure, giving the house a totem quality. The exterior stucco paint and the door and window trim were matched to the barks of surrounding fir trees. The walls were extended up past the roof, like arms reaching to the sky.* LEFT *The totem was carved by Terry Campbell of the Tsimshian tribe.* FAR LEFT *Poured-concrete platforms and expansive walls of windows are used to expand the house into the landscape. At left, a covered built-in grill allows for year-round outdoor cooking.*

When the house was under construction, the architect, the builder, and the owners carefully tied a small tree back and away from the structure. Once the walls went up, the tree was released to gently brush the window outside the bath.

The tree-tying ceremony serves as an allegory for how the Barnes's house in Nanaimo on Vancouver Island, British Columbia, was conceived and built and also for how it is lived in. Form follows passion; and here passion is for nature. From the broad expanse of the sea, to the native trees, to the distant coastal mountains, to the delicate lace of lichen on rock outcroppings, the house is a focal point for the elements, considered as essential to the living experience as food and water.

When Dave, a psychiatrist specializing in community mental health, and Fran, a retired landscape architect, decided to build on Nanaimo in the early 1990s, they instinctively knew that any house they built had to be a paean to nature. They completed the strenuous screening process of becoming a client of Patkau Architects in Vancouver, B.C., one of the most cutting-edge, controversial, and intuitively inspired firms in the world. Patkau agreed to work with the Barneses and set about conceiving an innovative design that would be so continuous with the natural world that before it even left the blueprints the house began to receive international design awards.

Set in the V-shaped cleft between two large mossy granite rocks, the browlike canopy and high parapet walls of the house refer to the totem poles of Pacific Coast natives. The solid walls soon melt into glass. Windows and doors with views of the Strait of Georgia and surrounding nature are framed in fir stained in a shade painstakingly matched to the bark of surrounding arbutus trees.

The 2,600-square-foot house is contemporary, the floor plan open, and the look sophisticated, but the label of "progressive architecture" stops here. Structural logic was tossed out for a look that's improvisational, irregular, and voluptuous, just like the house's natural setting. The Barnes house both embraces nature through views and mirrors her shapes and forms. Poured-concrete columns with black steel

ABOVE *A view of the forest floor from a small work space.*
LEFT *The lead-colored sculptural wall in the foreground is actually a door, closing the bedroom off from the living area. To the left, maple dining area cabinets were designed by the architect.*

branches emerging from their shapes grip the ceiling like muscular arms, recalling the scale and shapes of the surrounding forest. The placement of windows, some low, one tucked away at earth level downstairs, allow for the poetic dimension of natural light to play as large a role as the furnishings. Walls are skewed at different angles to capture views and moonscapes, the polished concrete floors were poured without two parallel seams, and the pleated fir canopy ceiling changes planes five times, undulating through the open space like a ribbon riding a breeze.

From the lower-level entrance, the expansive volume of the house is first seen from the space where the upper concrete floor has been cut back to allow for a wide stair with poured concrete risers. The white walls rise two and a half stories to the rich, red-gold tones of the wood ceiling. At the top of the stairs, a dazzling panorama of the sea appears from a northern view.

The upper level consists of the main living space, contained in one open room, with wide glass doors that pivot open, dissolving the walls. The master bedroom is separated from the public area by a set of maple storage cabinets and an elaborately designed sculptural door that notches into the opposite wall. Natural light in the sleeping space is filtered through skylights over the exposed roof joints, where moonscapes present an enigmatic drama of shapes and forms.

There is a precise beauty in the design and a clarity in details. Materials, strong and unembellished, reveal their naked beauty in concert with the serenity and spontaneity of nature, which plays the liveliest role in the design. "Living like this changes you forever, the way you see things, everything relating to everything else," says Fran. "We open the doors and windows, and birds find their way in here frequently." Dave is more succinct. "Every day when I return from work, it is like a holiday."

ABOVE *Three steel-encased concrete columns support the heavy timbered roof.* RIGHT *The entry level houses a studio for Fran's office and Dave's wood sculpting and Haida carving. Up the three steps are the guest quarters, the only area of the house that can be made completely private.* FAR RIGHT *The open living area achieves a balance of voluptuous discipline. Light filters in through skylights over exposed roof joists.*

LEFT *A seamless image of the outdoors in the master bath.* RIGHT *The architects describe the house as like a* camera obscura, *focusing a series of carefully framed views of nature from within.* BELOW *The experience of varying textures begins at the entry. The upper floor is cut back to make a wide opening for the elegant open-tread stairway. A pair of low windows frames moss-covered rocks. Views of the forest replace bathroom mirrors, upper cabinets for a desk, and solid entry walls.*

EAST MEETS WEST

Asian Echoes within a Rugged Spirit

As the gateway to the Pacific Rim, the Pacific Northwest receives the first echoes of its beauty, be it exotic or humble. Yet Asia's material offerings are only a fraction of its allure. ❧ Whether it is through the growing practice of Buddhism in the Northwest, the increasing interest in feng shui, or a desire for the contemplative garden, spirit is what unites us with the East. We have long understood that the true living experience comes not from controlling nature but from *immersion* in nature. ❧ The Eastern concepts of spare, graceful lines in design; open-room floor plans; and the use of humble everyday objects to adorn our homes are all natural characteristics of Regional style. Order and harmony, whether they're achieved by using colors and textures that mirror nature or by enjoying the clean, empty space of a traditional Eastern room, offer respite from our hectic lives. ❧ Some of the most sensual and calming pleasures of a home are the simplest: a bed on the floor, a centerpiece of peeled bark, the repetitive pattern of a shoji screen, a water feature that lulls us to sleep like a whispered haiku. ❧ The homes on these pages reflect the Northwest approach to simplicity, harmony, and our enduring reverence for nature as we bow to the tradition, style, and spirit of the East, whether it be in our architecture, in our interiors, or in a simple detail.

Strong geometric shapes are juxtaposed with rounded shapes and natural elements. The Ershig house, designed by Seattle architect George Suyama, is composed of a number of straight lines and right angles. It reflects the perfection of detail, subtle match of hues, and uncluttered elegance of Japanese-influenced design.

Tom Bender and Lane deMoll's Neahkahnie Cottage

Ask architect Tom Bender what the single most important design element is, and he answers without hesitation, "love." He's not paying homage to the 1960s; he really walks his talk. "My intent is always first to create a place with soul." The homes he designs for "ordinary folks" incorporate his three guiding principles: "There's chi, or life force, which is also the energy of a place, li, which is the intent behind the design, and tummy, which means trust your heart, your gut feelings." For years, he has been guided by the principle that it is energy, not matter, that creates space.

Tom has studied sacred spaces and specifically feng shui, the art and science of placing objects to achieve harmony with the environment, since 1970. In 1965 he studied architecture in Japan on a Rockefeller grant and was attracted to the culture's reverence for power spots. He remembers in particular the Kiyomizu Temple: its construction was nearly impossible but was warranted by the sacred space beneath.

Today, along with designing homes, he writes extensively on sacred spaces, creating shrines, and the philosophy and practice of feng shui.

His own home is nestled in between Neahkahnie Mountain and the Pacific Ocean on the Oregon coast. Appropriately, Neahkahnie means "place of the gods," and it was through a kind of divine intervention that Tom and his wife Lane deMoll found it. While living in Portland, the couple visited the coast for a day's hiking trip and came upon the homesite. "It was like the finishing piece of a jigsaw puzzle," Tom explains. "We were totally drawn to the land."

Plans were immediately underway for the 1,200-square-foot cottage that followed the principles of feng shui. Tom points out, for example, that the strong yang (male energy) of the ocean is balanced by the quiet yin (female energy) of the landscaping and house. A sliding wooden door fashioned with a gnarled root handle opens to an interior shoji screen. According to the philosophy of feng shui, the screens afford the entry privacy from both the exterior and the inside living area. Fronting the screens is a wooden wall of recycled chicken coops, the

ABOVE *The cottage has clear cedar-shingle siding and a large "mouth" to breathe in the Pacific Ocean air.* FAR LEFT *The gnarled root door handle was found on the beach below. Tom crafted the shoji screens to keep the entry separate from the living space, an important principle of feng shui.*

LEFT *Embellishments and furnishings are minimal. Nature provides the artwork.* BELOW *The wood stove, made from a recycled automobile engine block, warms the house.* RIGHT *Stones, flowers, bark, and other objects found in nature comprise the centerpiece of the spool table, where family and friends dine. Seating is on the floor, a platform raised slightly to define the space.*

wood aged to a deep red with golden hues. The wood stove is a recycled automobile engine block, puffing out enough heat to warm the house.

The Asian philosophy of living simply and in harmony with nature has always made intuitive sense to the Bender/deMoll family. The principles of feng shui take their cues from nature and bring the connection to nature indoors. Much of the philosophy of feng shui also concerns what is *not* seen—or heard. Harsh noises represent sha, or negative energy. Quiet takes priority. There is no television in this house, and even a refrigerator is deemed too noisy. A cupboard that opens from a kitchen corner wall to the outdoors through a series of small holes keeps food cool.

Furnishings are kept simple as well. The family sits on floor cushions to dine around a halved electrical cable spool. The bed is a low futon on the floor. All together, their furnishings would not fill up the average American den; only the chi is abundant.

Marilyn Higginson's Barn in Rural Oregon

You might find her in the pasture "texturing" metal lampshades with her .22 rifle. She likes the way the bullets make gentle bumps on the steel surface. Artist Marilyn Higginson is resourceful, creative, and easily at home on the vast landscape of unconventionality. Her house, a 4,200-square-foot corrugated metal barn, is a case in point.

It all started when she was scanning building magazines and came across advertisements for barns. The moment was epiphanous: she could afford a metal barn, complete most of the interior work on her own, and house herself and her studio under one roof. She ordered the barn package to be delivered to her Sheridan, Oregon, property, got some assistance with the trusses and with setting the windows and poles, and went to work constructing the interiors. It became a frontier loft on a twenty-acre retreat, an escapist's dream.

The barn is homely, completely lacking in the lyrical roof lines and weathered wood that have made American barns the subjects of paintings and photographs for decades. But the interiors are as unexpected as the wild turkeys that stalk Marilyn for corn handouts and court their own images in the shiny bumper of her car.

Japanese simplicity, in particular the philosophy of wabi-sabi, has influenced Marilyn's own art and interiors. Wabi-sabi is both a way of life and an aesthetic ideal. The philosophy at its heart is to strip away all that is unnecessary and to coax beauty out of ugliness. All truths come from the ephemera of organic nature, and imperfections impart the greatest beauty of all. "It makes more sense to me than anything else," Marilyn says.

Red origami birds fly from the fifteen-foot ceiling; the cinnabar-colored bath is made with recycled wood and designed like a Japanese teahouse. Smooth stones define the border of the bath, and every interior object is refined, elegant, and spare. Yet the barn exudes emotional warmth.

Being an artist as well as a craftsperson, Marilyn turns found objects into art and junk materials into furnishings. One side of the barn is fashioned in thick display shelves made from particle board. She sanded the wood to achieve a pattern like that found in nature, then

ABOVE *The barn's unrefined exterior and muddy color make the interior effect more profound.* LEFT *Detail of a deer, Marilyn's closest neighbor.* RIGHT *Marilyn designed the coffee table, a bone white set of rocks atop a stream of cracked white earthenware, covered in glass. The artistic technique is modeled after* kare sansui, *a Japanese term for a dry landscape in which water and erosion have sculpted the land.*

長田
辻川

applied lacquer to form a rich patina, similar to that found in Asian bowls and vessels. In the kitchen, she has cast thick black concrete countertops with textured edges. A Japanese folk cloth hangs at the edge of the kitchen as a mere suggestion of a room divider. Marilyn left the concrete floor a natural gray, allowing it to disappear.

Marilyn approaches the process of creating a home in the same way she creates her art—by practicing an ongoing, organic, and intimate way of reducing the psychic distance between herself and her environment—the way of wabi-sabi.

ABOVE *The shower chair is a basalt boulder. The Japanese bath represents a symbolic landscape in which stones are as important as plants.* LEFT *Marilyn's decor consists of objects that are understated yet impart a quiet authority. An indigo antique folk cloth from Japan hangs above the kitchen.* FAR LEFT *Marilyn's painting of clay sake bottles hangs above the range. She designed the kitchen, including the stove top, a geometric abstraction in steel.*

Peter and Deanna Birch's House on the Columbia River

ABOVE *The house received the Portland chapter of the American Institute of Architects' Honor Award, in part for its exquisite proportion, materials, and details.* LEFT *An expansive view of the river through a floor-to-ceiling curtain wall of glass with shoji proportions. A Le Corbusier chaise and a telescope make for spare, but essential, furnishings.*

It is a house of strength and presence, and one that reflects the pleasing marriage of Asian aesthetics and Northwest geography. Peter and Deanna Birch's home on the massive bluffs overlooking the Columbia River near Vancouver, Washington, is a classic example of how well East and West can come together.

A two-story, magnolia-colored, stucco-and-wood-clad Modernist box, the river-view house has a floor-to-ceiling glass wall system with black metal surrounds that suggest the exquisite proportions of a shoji. The glass, along with a pale palette, creates a space that captures light and views and allows for the shifting geometries that occur with different elevations of the house.

The interiors are a clean stroke of brevity in decor and subtlety in materials: maple and stainless accents and smooth Sheetrocked walls finished in painstaking paint selections that ultimately produced a taupe granite shade. The color keeps the space from looking too cold, a common flaw in minimalist designs.

Rick Potestio was the architect who spoke most clearly to the Birchs' simple, yet precise, needs. "Rick had a feel for the setting, for how the house should flow," says Deanna. "He knows contemporary architecture well, and he has respect for Asian culture."

Deanna was born in Japan and raised in several areas of Southeast Asia. "I grew up with simplicity. I am drawn to yin and yang, I need a very clean, very balanced look," she says.

When the architect began the Birchs' project, he had Mies van der Rohe's Barcelona Pavilion in mind. "The simple stacked concept of the pavilion allowed us to express the Japanese flavor of the house without being 'Japanesque,' " he says. "I love classical architecture—it's still the highest form, perfected over the centuries. But I like the Asian feeling that a house doesn't have to be symmetrical or grand and that the classical elements are still subordinate to the landscape. The movement of the house takes you right to the water."

An ordered simplicity is essential to the Birchs' state of mind. "Ever since I was a kid I've been very organized, and I still believe clean, simple lines—like an Armani dress—work best for everything, even mental health," Deanna says.

With such dramatic views, windows were one of the most critical design elements. Fabricated aluminum channels keep the glazing from looking too flat and give the house a sense of geometry. "Windows become too big here in the Northwest," says Potestio. "They can go beyond a human scale and stop inviting you in."

As a flight attendant traveling between Portland and Asia, Deanna has access to the most beautiful furnishings in the world, but she is a decor minimalist. "You should walk into a house and see the house, never the furniture," she says. "It's more peaceful."

ABOVE *A strong sense of entry is essential to Asian-influenced design. The Birch house meets the street with an austere but welcoming series of planes. A front gate leads to an interior courtyard and water feature.* RIGHT *A Buddha rests on a maple divider.* FAR RIGHT *Interiors are a monochromatic understatement, both in materials and furnishings.*

Billee and Herb Ershig's Bellingham House

Billee and Herb Ershig's home is so geometrically pure, so meticulously detailed, so palpably serene, that any fussy furnishing, any clumsy clutter, any interloper objet, would almost certainly cause it to shriek and fling itself into Bellingham Bay. Fortunately, the Ershigs have achieved a balance of style and livability that keeps decor to a minimum and spares the design from aesthetic angst.

Seattle architect George Suyama designed the Ershigs' home using two box structures in the classical proportions of a grid to achieve a total living space of 3,500 square feet. The larger box, containing the living area, is skewed at five degrees from the smaller box, which houses the garage and workshop. This slivered angle pulls a thread of tension through the tautly tuned structure, making the house more humanistic and adding a sensual dimension to the design.

Japanese in its subtlety, the Ershigs' home exposes architectural elements as an essential part of the overall aesthetic. Exposed I-beams and roof trusses make the structure part of the architectural elements, which is especially pleasing to Herb, a retired mechanical engineer. "I see the architecture as art," he says.

An exterior reflecting pool that meets the outside living room wall casts an abstract play of light and shadow on the room's ceiling, creating an almost ethereal calm. The street-level entry opens onto a mezzanine that looks down on the living and dining area, split by a floating stair. Materials provide an essay on textures and infuse the house with a graceful refinement. Cedar-channel siding is used inside and out, a subtle nuance of boundary blurring. Vertical-grain fir was used in doors and window trim. The kitchen's rift-cut white oak cabinets are an elegant contrast to the Norwegian slate countertops and polished aluminum light fixtures. Floors are laid in smooth two-foot squares of precast colored concrete pavers in a pale shade of taupe. There is a psychological component to living in such ordered harmony, with objects so precisely placed that even the television rises out of the hearth like a great surreal eye. This kind of harmony forces neatness. "I can't afford to make a mess," Billee laments. "It would drive me crazy."

ABOVE *The reflecting pond provides a play of shadow and light on the adjoining living room ceiling.* RIGHT *The bridge to the front entrance.* FAR RIGHT *The polished aluminum light fixtures were designed by the architect and built by Herb Ershig, who left the cords slightly bent "with memory."*

Liberman The Artist In His Studio
the Pageant of Painting
VENICE The Art of Living
THE ART OF RENE LALIQUE
GREAT PAINTINGS
FLAIR ANNUAL 1953
ALFRED STIEGLITZ
SILVER
GEORG JENSEN
SILVER in AMERICA
HISTORY OF ART BY H.W. JANSON
COLOR
SON OF HEAVEN

LEFT *The home's self-contained upper living quarters reflect the intimacy and privacy typical of many Japanese homes.* FAR LEFT *Seattle designer Judy Davison specified or designed many of the couple's furnishings. The monochromatic tones and balance of textures ensure that pieces enhance, not overwhelm, the architecture.*

ABOVE *The bedroom's serenity is enhanced by a view of Bellingham Bay.* LEFT *The powder room sink is made of cast silver and bronze and was designed by David Gulassa of Seattle. The wall behind the mirror is painted plywood overlain with a layer of smoked bronze Plexiglas. The countertops are a thick slab of poured concrete.* RIGHT *A view of the living room from the upper level. The large painting on the back wall is by artist Leo Adams.*

5

Urban Dwelling

Sublime City Sanctuaries

We don't all dream of hiking trails, sailboats, and compost piles. Fog-lifting lattes, city skylines, and evenings at the symphony inspire some of us. Urbanites' leisure pursuits run from poetry jams to tastings at brew pubs. If we want nature, we'll read about it in a book. ⁓ Seattle urbanites revel in their eight acres of Pioneer Square. Full of refurbished architectural gems, the section rose from the ashes after a fire destroyed the city's first commercial buildings in 1889. Now the Richardian Romanesque low-rises house a hive of chic coffee bars washed in umber and black, and busy bookstores, where plump chairs draw browsers to drop in and read until closing. Just east of the square is the International District, a flourishing Asian community with some of the best bakeries, shops, and pan-Asian cuisine in the Northwest. Pike Place Market, a turn-of-the-century marketplace, is a chock-a-block placement of stylish shops and stalls crammed bazaarlike into seven acres of harbor front. Street performers are omnipresent, though the rain fills their hats faster than the coins do. Locals and tourists roam the red brick streets and

Figuero has claimed one of the arched windows that face the Portland skyline. The Persian goddesses, Lily and Iris, are made of cement, newspaper, and plaster and came from Portland's now defunct Oriental Theater.

ABOVE *The silver mercury vases and gazing balls are nineteenth century. When they're paired with white candles, elegance is instant, especially at night.* FAR RIGHT *Plastic pink flamingos add a dash of kitsch to a loft rooftop, belying the opulence that lies below.*

flower-lined alleys, trolling for the best of the region's bounty: fresh produce, decadent pastries, and just-caught fish hawked by wisecracking fishmongers who juggle fish and tempt the passersby: "get 'em while they're frish." Culture abounds. The Seattle Opera is now a premier national arts organization, chamber music is a local passion, and theater, including the acclaimed Seattle Repertory, is the city's weightiest culture card. ☙ No matter how strong the craving for concrete and chaos, going urban in Portland is still a green experience. Portland is a city of parks. It's impossible to stroll downtown, a mere thirteen by twenty-six compact blocks of extraordinarily insightful planning, and miss the shade of the old elms or the emerald swath of lawn dotted with benches and rose bushes. "The Pearl," an area of hyper urban renewal, zoned for both industrial and residential building, has been compared to New York City's SoHo district. Traditionally used for warehousing, the blocks are filled with old buildings, the tired logos of their earlier industrial tenants barely visible on the worn red brick. Now one of the area's most stylish urban residential scenes, the Pearl began as a handful of studio/lofts for artists until increasing property values and soaring rents made them a flight risk. As artists find cheaper real estate elsewhere in the city, the Pearl thrives on young professionals, empty nesters, and the relentlessly hip. ☙ Loft living, though not new, became increasingly popular in the Pacific Northwest by the mid nineties. The reasons, according to the owners, are simple: feet or bicycles make for cheap transportation, the best food in the region is around the corner, and the cultural life, much of it dirt cheap, serves up the best of the city minus the hassle of finding a parking place. ☙ This chapter introduces four urban dwellings, two in Seattle and two in Portland, whose dwellers find it's the urban heart that beats the strongest.

May and Wah Lui's Urban Studio

ABOVE *The rooftop terrace is used for entertaining, a playground, and reading the morning paper.* LEFT *The central living area is a minimalist's dream. The Luis are clear-minded about the use of space in their loft. The spacious main floor was designed for family and entertaining, the upper level as a private and intimate sanctuary.*

Just when it seems safe to peg Pacific Northwesterners as the quintessential nature lovers, enter the Luis. "I couldn't care less if I ever see a body of water—or a mountain," says Wah Lui without apology. Both originally from China, May and Wah have made Seattle their home since high school. Downtown Seattle satisfies the couple's urban fervor, fueled by their proximity to the city's cultural events and work (their studio is a seven-minute drive from their home). They own several photography studios throughout the Pacific Northwest. Wah Lui photographs the Seattle Opera, among other cultural performances, and the couple entertains frequently. Fund-raising dinners include their own music festivals for the arts, held in their loft.

From the street below, their 5,000-square-foot loft sits boldly like a foil dome loomed over by its behemoth neighbors—residential, office, and civic high-rises. The outside of the loft, corrugated steel, was selected for its slick price. Wah told Seattle architect Gerald Kumata to "do the exterior in something cheap because I'll never look at the outside." Kumata conceded but didn't sacrifice style in the process.

Up the narrow elevator accessed through a gritty garage, the doors open to a huge, active space where a grand piano sits idle until the next concert/dinner party. Steel columns encased in paper and rounding out at two feet in diameter are actually supports for the thirty-foot ceiling. A wall of windows faces the urban core like an unblinking eye trained on Seattle. The light changes constantly, the silhouette reflecting the colors of the sky and landscape and the expressions of the city's urban face, like a Chuck Close painting.

The floors are wood planks, the walls are painted Tuscan yellow, and the columns are encased in a textured paper painted the color of a sun-dried tomato. Despite the Italian hues, the space is imbued with a feminine roundness and quietude that is subtly Asian. "We didn't tell Gerry to design it Oriental, but I think it subconsciously came through," says May.

The couple have traveled extensively, and many of their furnishings were acquired on trips—the French Empire sofa, the Beidermeier

ABOVE *A sculpture by a Boston artist rests against a paper-encased column.* LEFT *Spaces are kept clear, giving the Luis' daughter a clear path to roller-skate. The master bedroom above has a city view through the loft and onto the Seattle skyline.* RIGHT *A photograph of dancer and choreographer Martha Graham hangs behind an antique English game table. The Luis found the companion chairs at a San Francisco antique fair. An English tea service rests upon the table's leather top, ready for the daily ritual of afternoon tea.*

bench, a wood sculpture by a Boston artist, a Rosenthal table spotted in Paris. But they make it clear that everything has a function; nothing just sits around looking good. "One rule," says Wah, "is if it's here, it's got to be used."

Two things escape the Luis' rule of utility: the parrots, Jordan and Tosca, and the art. Photographs hung low on the walls line the loft. Some are by famous photographers such as Imogene Cunningham and Diane Arbus. Others are outside the collective, their photographers unknown. Wah makes it clear he is no art collector. "I look for the image, never the photographer," he says.

The Collector's Loft

The owner spent years on the East Coast, so it's no surprise that he led the loft movement in Portland's Pearl District. The area, one of gritty warehouses and office buildings, is zoned for both commercial and residential use and casts the template for living among Portland's growing art scene. This former machine shop became an ideal spot from which to walk to restaurants and entertainment. Seduced by the ceiling, a dramatic canopy of old-growth timber columns with exposed joists and blocking, the owner bought the building in the late seventies. He waited a few years, though, living in the suburbs, before his yen for urban life drew him into loft living. Architect Edgar Wilson Smith and designer Ralph Cereghino helped him to convert the warehouse into 6,000 square feet of living space.

Painting and sculpture from the sixties dominate the important collection, which the owner acquired on the East Coast, where he was an art student. He began buying contemporary art soon after he graduated from college. Dense arrangements of artworks and kitschy collections are mounted side by side—an ideal solution for a collector who seems to possess an unending enthusiasm for many forms of visual expression. Major works include those by contemporary artists such as Andy Warhol, Jeff Koons, David Salle, Frank Stella, and other abstract painters who anticipated the new conceptual avant-garde in the 1950s and 1960s. So sophisticated is the collection that it risks being above and beyond any reference to Portland. Saving it from pure reverence are the owner's junk-shop and flea-market finds: dozens of whimsical ceramic cookie jars, can art made from tin cans ("Can't you see all those housewives creating this? They were the original recyclers"), dozens of wind-up tin toys from the 1800s, and intricate tramp-art boxes carved by post-Civil-War itinerants.

The furnishings are simple, classic. The owner possesses a rare George Nelson marshmallow sofa and Knoll chairs designed by Charles Pollock, the latter spied at a garage sale. "I like their utility," the owner says. "They're not fussy, they're just functional."

ABOVE *Portland's Pearl district has been compared to New York's SoHo district. Dozens of trendy bistros, tiny cafes, art galleries, and chic boutiques line the streets.* RIGHT *A Frank Stella aluminum sculpture,* Hawaiian Shearwater, *dominates the back wall. The glass coffee table was designed by Noguchi. The 1950s sofa was recently re-covered in off-white chenille. The owner liked it so much that he had a companion sofa made.*

WET DRY

LEFT *Fifteen-foot-high walls on the second-story living space accommodate the large canvases and sculptures. Italian glass vases dress the dining table, a 1956 Omega design by Hans Eichenberger. The vacuum cleaners are sculptures by artist Jeff Koons that came out of the Neo-Geo school of the eighties. The horse is by Deborah Butterfield.* BELOW *Andy Warhol's* Jackie *hangs across from a Helen Frankenthaler canvas. The wall credenza is made of formed plastic, an early piece by Raymond Loewy.*

ABOVE *Duane Hanson's sculpture,* The Dishwasher, *molded from a living form and cast in resin, is so lifelike that it gives visitors a jolt. The painting is* Golden Days *by Kenneth Noland.* RIGHT *The collection of cookie jars rests on commercial stainless-steel shelving. A Charles Eames lounge chair awaits a quiet afternoon of reading. The Eero Saarinen tulip chairs and pedestal table form the perfect place for breakfast when terrace weather is too wet or too cold.* FAR RIGHT *The entry-level wall is further defined by a Haim Steinbach sculpture. Above left, a Carroll Dunham canvas leads to the loft's upstairs living area.*

Michael Coy and Michael Brasky's Seattle Condominium

What do you do when you have more style than money and more taste than time? You buy a small apartment in an early-1920s brick building a block from Seattle's Volunteer Park. Hopefully, the building will go condominium. Hopefully, you can afford it.

Next, you begin a story about this small space, a narrative filled with irony, elegance, and humor, and one that always builds toward a new twist in the plot.

That is what Michael Coy and Michael Brasky, owners of M. Coy Books in Seattle, did. Both former Portlanders, they were committed urbanites who moved to Seattle in 1981. Ten years later they opened the Pike Place Market-area business, a casual and inviting space that smells of fresh coffee and the intrigue of books.

When he's not helping bibliophiles browse, which is rare, Michael Brasky prowls the city for antiques and art, junk and *junque*-retro toys, game pieces, books, croquet balls, lacquer boxes, baskets, and furniture—things that were discarded because people don't yet know that bowling balls, placed right, become sculpture.

The condominium is small and intimate. Neighbors' profiles in an adjacent window are close enough to determine lipstick shades. The space looks like a cross between a movie set for a French poet and the pied-à-terre of an eccentric American who is only days away from having his desire to collect diagnosed as a disease. Fine art, such as works by Royal Nebeker, Petra Mathers, and Marsha and Michael Burns, slides in among flea-market finds. A red lacquer box holds a collection of colored pencil sharpeners. A blue bowl holding fresh lemons sits on a stack of books, and antique urns hold wooden croquet balls. Masks from an old general store line the walls, watching over dinner guests. There are three thousand books. The cats have to dive for free space.

The apartment is a voyeur's delight, a feast for the curious, a lair of beautiful bibelots, a temple of enshrined kitsch. Guests enter a tiny museum of treasures that span decades and sometimes centuries. "I aim for perfection, then try to screw it up a bit," says Brasky. "But some people walk in and just don't get it."

ABOVE *Seattle's Volunteer Park contains some of the city's finest architectural gems. The neighborhood has a dynamic mixture of people and a strong cultural draw, such as the Asian Art Museum.* FAR LEFT *An old library table in the entry displays porcupine quill boxes from Ceylon. Humpty Dumpty is part of a children's book department display from the 1920s. A "bouquet" of posters, collected from the last twenty-five years of book conventions, fills a jade-green, hand-thrown pottery umbrella stand.*

ABOVE *Dogs are a ubiquitous presence in this condominium, in myriad forms. An innocent interest became an earnest collection-turned-obsession. Friends often bring canine art as gifts for their surrendering hosts.* LEFT *The dining table is a teak square, painted black after a bottle of shoe polish changed its karma.* RIGHT *The pea-green Naugahyde chairs in the sitting room are from the fifties. The Adirondack table is stacked with books, bowls, and spheres.*

PAPER
PAPER
LAURA GILPIN An Enduring Grace

THE ILIAD OF HOMER
THE SHELL
THE SUN KING
MADAME DE POMPADOUR
MARY RENAULT
MAX PERKINS
TED MORGAN
Letters of E.B.White
TOO STRONG FOR FANTASY
THE RECKONING
North American Indian Art
OPEN SEASON
HOW WAR CAME
Lisle Letters
COCTEAU
BOB WOODWARD
The Saddest Story
THE DOG IS US
THIRTEEN DAYS
Kennedys
Desolate Angel
TIMEBENDS
Lost Friendships
HERSELF

LEFT *The French candelabras on the coffee table are nineteenth century, gifts to the men for helping a friend move. Native American baskets, many beautifully asymmetrical, are part of a collection gathered over twenty-five years.* RIGHT *The kitchen is whimsical, with Fiestaware cramming the shelves. The cotton tablecloth, found at a garage sale, bears a Mexican fiesta scene. The iron ice cream chairs have seats fashioned from the wood of an old Frederick and Nelson department store candy counter.*

S. LIBENSKY
J. BRYCHTOVA

Denise and Larry Grimes's Portland Loft

The Grimeses are always bringing something home: Persian goddesses, paper cocoons, oversized eggs, armfuls of fresh flowers, friends. They were one of the pioneering couples of Portland's residential loft movement, first trying out loft life in the early 1980s. Having run the gamut from the hideous to the passable, they've finally wound up with the sublime. Their 2,400-square-foot space has air-conditioning, a wall of arched windows that faces the urban core, a freight elevator that opens to their bedroom, and even a communal cat, Figuero.

The couple are committed urbanites; evenings they can be found at a neighborhood Pearl District restaurant, the theater, an art gallery, or at home grilling up succulent vegetables grown on their rooftop garden. Both Denise and Larry work downtown—she is a fashion consultant, he is a chef and owns Art of Catering. Larry spends his off-hours on his own art, sculptural works crafted from clay, wood, and found objects.

Living among the artists of the early Pearl era fueled the couple's growing interest in art and was the genesis of their collection of contemporary art. Following the careers of emerging artists and occasionally trading culinary masterpieces for painting and sculpture has enabled the Grimeses to collect great works on a budget. "We never thought about collecting," says Denise. "It just unfolded with the way we lived." Their art tends toward the sculptural, in part, says Larry, because the three dimensions work well in the huge open spaces and break up the big block of space.

Both Denise and Larry are active in their neighborhood association, taking on missions from getting more than one television station ("I *know* the local weather," says Larry) to increasing safety on the streets. One of the more popular projects is Almost Free Cinema, an idea borrowed from Seattle's Fremont neighborhood. For a buck, locals can pull up a chair or plop down a pillow, pop open the cooler, light the hibachi, then sit back and enjoy the show. A retro double feature is shown on the gritty brick wall of the chosen building.

ABOVE *Color, texture, art, and irony make the Grimeses' loft unique. The man standing on his head is by artist Rick True.* FAR LEFT *To create asymmetrical living spaces, the Grimeses created partial walls of staggered heights. The "egg" sculpture on the floor by Pittsburgh, Pennsylvania, artist Carol Humata is titled* The Half of It. *Also by Humata is the wire cage on the cantaloupe-colored wall called* Double Negative.

ABOVE *Larry's conical metal and found-object sculptures are in the foreground.* RIGHT *Denise and Larry refurbished the dining chairs, which they found at an upscale Seattle junk shop. The painting is by Portland artist Italia LaRuffa.* FAR RIGHT *The kitchen is small, yet amazing culinary masterpieces emerge from this space. Larry found the letters in an Atlanta, Georgia, antique shop.*

KITCHEN
Montague GRIZZLY

6

Artists, Writers, Cooks, and Visionaries

At Home with Free Spirits

The dining room curtains are plain white silk fabric tied in loose knots at the center, modeled after the peasant windows of Prague. The old dining table is from Mexico, crafted by Russian Mennonites. The copper light fixture, originally a gaslight, was wired for electricity. Artist friend Terry Siebert made the apple bowls.

It is axiomatic to say that creative people live in creative homes, yet how that creativity is expressed is what makes the dwellings in this chapter so exciting. It is also a comment on the Northwest spirit that one can revive a prune dryer, a log cabin, a Swedish farmhouse, or a former dance hall without a moment's thought that these structures, at least in the condition in which they were found, might be the slightest bit impractical to live in. But whether it's hand building a cave, crafting almost all one's own furniture, or ripping out thirty years' growth of blackberry vines to plant a garden, it's all in a day's—or decade's—work. The style in these pages is eccentric, passionate, witty, clever, and sure to break the rules of formal design. ❧ This chapter reveals people, who, it's safe to say, color outside the lines. Their homes are as unique, fascinating, and delightful as they are.

PASTORAL PARADISE

Haje Boman's Nineteenth-Century Swedish Farmhouse in Helvetia

This Oregon heirloom is a survivor. It began as a humble Swiss farmhouse in 1875, the haven of Scandinavian labor settlers who built the two-bedroom Victorian and began to tend the land of other farmers. Situated on sixteen acres in Helvetia ("Switzerland" in Swedish), a farming community near Portland, it's had its trials. One owner tried to burn the place down to collect insurance money. A 1960s commune nearly let it fall into ruin. That didn't faze Swedish-born Haje Boman, who, after buying the farmhouse in 1992, suffered her own trials. A harsh 1996 winter pressed the barn into near collapse, and the flood of 1997 picked it up and dropped it flat, finally ending its days. (Haje used the weathered wood to face the stalls of the new barn.)

Haje was living in New York when she read a book on the Pacific Northwest and fell in love with Oregon. She was especially enthralled by the farmlands. She traded in city life as an antiques dealer for the pastoral setting and twelve-hour days restoring her farmhouse. Though the house needed endless hours of work, the location was like a postcard: perfect, idyllic. Three full growing seasons cause the Helvetia hills to be swabbed in a riot of colors, shapes, and textures. Wheat, oats, red clover, crimson clover, and alfalfa are among the crops grown on neighboring farms.

Haje has restored the farmhouse as authentically as possible to reflect a traditional Swedish farmhouse. She avoided opening up interiors and adding on to keep the house true to its modest origin. Instead, she made each of the little niches and rooms into separate living areas with charming details and decor. She textured the walls and ceilings with a coat of stucco and painted several walls and wood trim in dark forest and fir greens, dark terra-cotta reds, and wheat. Tramp art, a collection of log cabins, candles, flowers, Amish quilts, Haje's woven textiles, hook rugs, Navajo rugs, and the art-and-craft work of her three children fill up the little farmhouse. The floor's original wide asymmetrical fir planks are polished and covered with area rugs.

Haje's loom, which she brought from Sweden, sits in the small sunroom off the dining area. She weaves rag rugs, blankets, towels, and

ABOVE *A bed of lavender, planted and harvested for gifts, marks an aromatic entry to the farmhouse. Wooden scalloped shingles on the gable ends of the farmhouse have been preserved.* FAR LEFT *Every window in the farmhouse has an idyllic view: Haje's gardens, the pond, pastoral farms, lyrical barns, and stands of Douglas fir. In the distance, the coastal mountain range makes an inspired setting.*

wall hangings but is emphatic about not calling herself a textile artist. "Weaving is a part of my heritage, it's integrated into my life, not a separate art," she says. Clumps of dried lavender (lavender grows only steps away in an impromptu garden near the home's entrance) hang over the loom. Every year Haje makes fresh potpourri, bed-sized lavender pillows, and sachets as gifts for friends and family.

The heart of the home is the room at the entry, where four simple wooden rockers sit facing the Rais woodstove, a Scandinavian design from the 1930s. The chairs symbolize Haje's connection to her three children. When each child was born, Haje acquired a rocker from which to nurse the baby. Later, each chair became the child's own heirloom. In evenings, the family gathers in front of the fire, each in his or her own chair, to talk, write, work on weavings, and tie fishing flies.

ABOVE *Balls of yarn sit on the floor below the Glimåkra loom, awaiting metamorphosis.* RIGHT *A filigreed balustrade, which Haje painted in tones of the surrounding natural setting, supports the carpeted fir treads leading to the upstairs bedrooms.* FAR RIGHT *An eleven-foot-long Swedish farm table, in Haje's family for three generations, is used for work projects and suppers. The Navajo red-and-white wall textile is from the 1890s.*

ABOVE *The bathroom was updated but kept simple. Haje made the sink stand from brass pipe and green Brazilian slate "which blends with anything in the Northwest." She also incorporated the Japanese practice of raising the water bowl above the surface, a technique she likes for aesthetic reasons.* RIGHT *Haje added stainless-steel countertops to the tiny kitchen. The countertops and the new fir green paint were the few kitchen updates.* FAR RIGHT *It took Haje a year to get a permit for the Swedish stove, which she ordered from her homeland. The style was rare here, but patience was rewarded with authenticity.*

W

Nance Schaefle and Estelline O'Harra's Portland House

The place was such a dump when they bought it in the late 1980s that, among other things, Nance Schaefle and Estelline O'Harra had to haul away eighty-four tires. But it was a divine dump, and the price was right: $57,000. As artists, they knew that with enough time, imagination, and sense of humor, they could restore the place.

Originally built in the early forties, the Portland-area house was soon torn down and rebuilt as a dance hall for locals who liked to two-step on Saturday nights. Coincidentally, the women's restoration efforts included laying a wood floor recycled from another old area dance hall. The narrow-plank maple floors still bear the deft traces of the jitterbug. "We thought it was a good omen," says Nance.

The result is a craftsman-style post-and-beam cabin, warmed by native woods, soft folk rugs and tablecloths, North-American antiques, and the women's own hand-crafted furniture: tramp art re-creations, Adirondack and hickory-style chairs, and desks and wildlife wood carvings. The look is mellow, charming, and woodsy, a rustic old East Coast hunting lodge with a dash of western wit.

The house is dark. Trees envelop the homesite, and the few windows let in only a sliver of light. Instead of cutting into walls, and worse, cutting down trees, the women turned the darkness into atmosphere through the use of amber light, toffee tones, and burnished woods. They painted the walls a pale tobacco shade, then lightly textured them, finishing with a rag-off technique and a final glazing to give them the sheen of a worn leather saddle. Other walls are vertical-grain fir panels. All the furnishings are wood: the meticulous carved and textured pieces crafted by Estelline, and the twigwork by Nance. The women design under the name of C.W. Pickets (the C. W. stands for cranky women) and sell their pieces to collectors who own resort lodges and fly fishing shops and to people who want to give their homes the look of an old East Coast Adirondack fishing camp. "We really pull together a kind of feeling more than anything," says Estelline. "I call it the lure of the lodge."

ABOVE *Cedar shingles, overhanging eaves, and green trim transformed the exterior of a run-down cabin into a small craftsman-style lodge.* FAR LEFT *The women use the covered front porch for displaying their collection of vintage American flags, antique rockers, birdhouses, and a twig game table. The overall look reflects the women's love of vintage Americana, a lovingly preserved piece of the past.*

RUSTIC

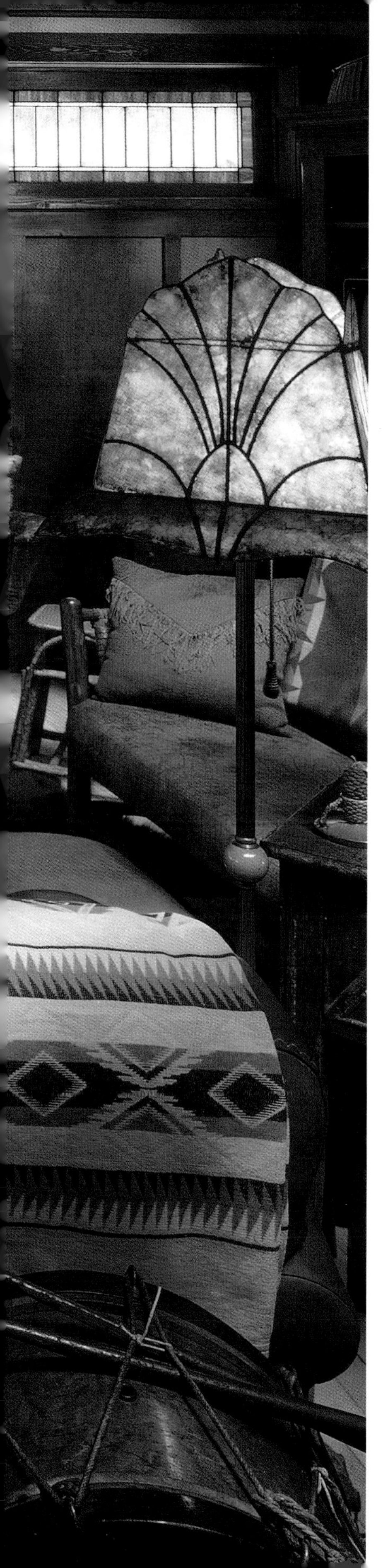

LEFT *The cabin's living room is bathed in amber light. The glass-front tramp art cabinet against the paneled wall was an old piece the women found in Canada and re-created with carved trim. The pony is a collector's piece carved by the late Oregon folk artist Fannie Branson.*
BELOW *Nance and Estelline re-created the old desk and chair by adding birch bark and carved wood trim. Nance says, "We give things another life."*

ABOVE *The showroom for C.W. Pickets creations was an addition to the house. The fir paneling, exposed beams, and craftsman-style windows make the addition appear seamless.* LEFT *The back deck of the cottage opens to three acres of large cedars, Douglas fir, and maple trees. The tablecloth is an old Pendleton child's bed blanket.* RIGHT *Bead board cabinets and a large collection of Greenware pottery celebrate an earlier era.*

Heidi Rickabaugh's Newberg Prune Dryer

ABOVE *The silolike feature at the top of the barn was once the vent for the prune dryer. The silo is now home to swallows that nest in the barn. The barn, painted in the Pennsylvania Dutch style of brick-red and white after its first conversion to a residence, was built at a slight angle to allow hot air to rise and dry the prunes and nuts.* FAR RIGHT *Salvaged architectural details give the farmhouse interiors a European look and feel. The baskets hanging from a ceiling beam were crafted by the couple's friends, Beth Peterson and Mark Kelz of Cave Junction, Oregon.*

They were looking to simplify their lives, and the house was looking for them. Heidi Rickabaugh recalls walking through the old place years ago, before her family was ready for country life. When it came on the market again more than a decade later, Heidi and her late husband, Robin, took a second look. "I suddenly remembered how much I had once loved the place," recalls Heidi. "I was starting to recognize it all over again—this time as our home."

Resting in an idyllic stretch of undulating gold and green farmland near Newberg, the old barn rises gently above the landscape like a sweet image from a child's dream. Converted to living space in 1977 by a previous owner, the barn was once a prune dryer. The Rickabaughs, though, have made folk art and flea markets a prune dryer's best bet for a divine comeback. Heidi, a graphic designer, owns and runs Principia Graphica, a company she and Robin spent years building into a successful graphic arts business. As graphic artists, book designers, and experts in image packaging, their working world was filled with artists, many of whom became close friends. Clay vessels, bowls, and sculptures are aesthetically pleasing but also serve as dinnerware, cookware, and vessels for flowers and fruits. Almost every fine craft also has a practical use, even if it's a nap stoop for the cat.

Old architectural details and fragments, such as pilasters and cornices, and antique lighting give the barn European style and satisfied Heidi's need to add a twist of irony to the barn's distinctly American tableau. Estate-sale finds and European antiques mix with a treasured collection of fine and Northwest folk art amassed over thirty years. Most of the furnishings are old family heirlooms, coaxed into another generation of service. The overall effect is one of bohemian comfort, what Heidi calls "our shabby chic."

German-born Heidi was drawn to the structure because, as in the European farmhouses of her childhood memories, the storage and utility area was at ground level and the living space was above, at eye level to the tree branches. "In Europe, the animals are kept below the living area, where they help to keep the farmhouse warm," she says.

A form of unbidden animal husbandry has found Heidi in this country. In the old prune dryer, swallows nest in the open wood stairwell leading up to the living area. Their numbers are swelling astronomically, lessening their charm. "We are trying to get them to practice family planning," says Heidi.

The big red barn is surrounded by ten acres of evergreens and fruit trees. When the couple moved in, Robin planted flowers and vegetables and began to cultivate a beautiful garden, giving the flavorful plums perpetuity and the deer a choice of meals. "We have gourmet deer here," explains Heidi. "They really prefer the roses."

ABOVE *The sculpture on the table of boys playing ball is by regional artist Russell Childers. The painting on the wall above is by Robin's brother, Rene Rickabaugh.* LEFT *Pansy the cat rests on a cluster of trees sculpted by George Kettlewell. The plums are fresh from the garden.* FAR LEFT *The kitchen is small but serviceable. An old plate rail makes a window valance. Artists George Kettlewell and Kersti Hamann created the crockery bowl in the foreground. The ceramic jars are by Connie Kiener.*

Carol Gardner's Sunriver House

ABOVE *Carol worked to painstakingly restore architectural aspects of pioneer life. Her efforts included commissioning veteran craftsmen for the ironwork, lighting, and masonry.*
LEFT *The Little Deschutes River, which meanders through the property, was planted with brown and rainbow trout to help restore the Old Homestead's flourishing natural habitat. The alpine meadow in the background receives several inches of snow each year, making cross-country skiing as close as the back door.*

At first it seems odd for the Northwest's queen of pop culture to live in a log cabin. Then she lets you know that she is a fourth-generation Oregonian, that she grew up around Native American reservations, and that she spends a good deal of time on horseback. Carol Gardner, author of the pop Americana primer *Bumper Sticker Wisdom* and the brain behind *Zelda Wisdom* greeting cards and accessories, spent a decade renovating and restoring the historical homesite. Now, she claims, the house is restoring her.

Nestled in a sweet curve of the Little Deschutes River, which cuts across an alpine meadow below the Cascade Mountains in central Oregon, the house was originally the home of the son of two of Oregon's first settlers, Jackson and Grace Clark Vandevert. William Plutarch Vandevert built a log house on the site, summoned his wife, Sadie, and their seven children from Texas, and settled into the place he called the Old Homestead. The Vandeverts abandoned the place in the 1950s.

Nearly a hundred years after the first log was laid, the timbers were rotting, the floors were collapsing, and the original mud chinking was loose. Carol, along with her former husband Jim Gardner, found herself rebuilding the house, raising it from the flood plain where it sat, and using the original template with indigenous lodgepole pine, stained and peeled to resemble the original logs by local craftsman Ed Adams. One of the most engaging artistic embellishments of the log house is the distinctive and original ironwork, created for the house during the restoration. Craftsman Russ Maugins, who created the ironwork for Oregon's iconic 1930s W. P. A. project, Timberline Lodge, was coaxed out of retirement to create iron details, including the home's chandeliers, a buffalo head door knocker, and the bent-arrow door handle on the front door. The guest house, now restored as a colorful western retreat for visiting friends, was once a cabin ordered from the Sears catalog.

The hefty size and strong horizontal lines of the logs give the house a brawny muscular feel. The interiors, shaggy and relaxed, respect the history of the place but depart from the feel of a humble homestead

LEFT *One of many antique saddles in the Old Homestead.* RIGHT *The massive fireplace is made of Camas basalt, a local rock. Zelda, tired after a photo shoot, relaxes in the foreground. The beaded dress is from the Yakima Indian tribe.* BELOW *Carol rides her pinto pony every morning or evening, often joining friends who board their horses at the Old Homestead. Views take in regional flora and fauna, including aspens, ponderosa pines, mule deer, osprey, and otters.*

with what Carol calls "western funkitude." Mechanical cowboys and horses mix with nineteenth-century furnishings and antiques. Cigar store Indians lurk in corners. Photos of Zelda, Carol's English bulldog, who will strike a pose as a has-been diva or don a headdress for her *Sitting Bull Dog* persona, are blown up to poster size.

Carol designed oversized peeled pine sofas and chairs, upholstering them with soft red-and-black-checkered Hudson's Bay blankets. George Lawrence saddles hang over stairway balustrades, Edward Curtis prints line the walls, and there are enough skins, heads, and antlers to give any game hunter trophy envy. As an artist and writer, Carol loved the rustic stateliness of the log house and acknowledges that it could be done "to the nines" in priceless early-American antiques and accessories. Her playful and endlessly busy imagination, though, kept her from the folderol of formality. "You can only go so far with respectable, stately," Carol explains. "It's an old log house. The image here explains the style."

ABOVE *Carol's bedroom overlooks an Alpine meadow, a ribbon of the Little Deschutes River, and ultimately the Cascade Mountains.* LEFT *Most of the pillows in the log house were made from old Pendleton blankets.* FAR LEFT *The bedroom was furnished with family heirlooms and antiques found in Portland shops.*

Woodleigh Marx Hubbard's Bainbridge Island Sanctuary

ABOVE *The large flower garden adds a significant element to Woodleigh's decor. Fresh flowers fill the house.* LEFT *Weather permitting, Woodleigh works outdoors at a number of creative perches, making art in a myriad of mediums under the rare grace of natural light.* FAR LEFT *The Northwest-style cedar cottage on five acres "has the soul of Robert Frost." The broad, overhanging porch eaves allow Woodleigh to extend the living area to the outdoors. Oriental and Native American rugs, sculptures, and chairs become part of the natural setting.*

For years Woodleigh Marx Hubbard was a vagabond. She lived in Paris, Manhattan, Denver—a dozen places, sleeping on mattresses on the floor, carting her art supplies, and little else, around on her nomadic journeys. The idea of being tethered to a house and all its responsibilities was fine—for other people. Then a friend practically shooed her into her house on Bainbridge Island, exclaiming, "Woodleigh, it's made for you!"

A thirty-five-minute ferry ride from Seattle, the island is home to artists, Seattle commuters, and longtime residents looking to shed some stress. Big gulls perch on supermarket grocery carts, gadget stores hold the allure of art galleries, and master gardeners have more secrets than the Pentagon. Here, Woodleigh has found the perfect setting: a wooded retreat where she can create, and, with the village only minutes away, society at her elbow.

Woodleigh describes first seeing the house as a magical experience. "It was just like a first kiss," she says. "I could never have imagined its sweetness until it actually happened to me."

Now settled, with contemporary furniture and things that smack of permanence, she is under the spell of the house, with its cricket songs and soft evening breezes. Simple and relaxed, with a surrounding

ABOVE *The painting is by Woodleigh. The view is to her back deck and the forest beyond.* FAR RIGHT *Fir-plank floors get a mix of sisal and Oriental rugs. Woodleigh painted the whimsical chest under the side table. A simple glass-topped cabinet serves as a coffee table and displays several of Woodleigh's published books.*

cedar-plank porch with round wooden columns, the house blends into its wooded setting as easily as the smile line on the bark of a tree. "It has the heart of Frank Lloyd Wright and the soul of Robert Frost," she says. "I want to stay here forever."

The design, in fact, is that of Bainbridge Island architect James Cutler, who designed the 1,200-square-foot single-story contemporary in the late 1970s.

The spare design and native materials create such a gentle relationship with the natural world that Woodleigh believes the house helps fuel her creativity. Large windows filter light onto the open floor plan and create views from which to watch the recycling seasons. A small U-shaped kitchen extends to an eating area under a large set of windows cut into the sloped ceiling.

When Woodleigh first settled, she had a futon and art supplies. "I needed a cupboard, so I made one," she says, pointing to a colorful primitive-inspired cabinet. "Then I needed dishes, so I made them and stored them inside." Mixed with Woodleigh's own art—she also writes and illustrates children's books—are paintings by her father, Earl Hubbard, and books by her mother, spiritual visionary and futurist Barbara Marx Hubbard. To help get the interiors pulled together, Woodleigh enlisted "the two hip island babes," Katrina McDermott and Katherine Fuerst, owners of Embellish!, a local interiors shop and service. The pair was drawn to Woodleigh's art and the challenge of her few, but eccentric, possessions. "We wanted the house to reflect Woodleigh, all her talent and color and exuberance," says Katherine. "Still, we needed to incorporate her personality *and* make the house functional."

Proof that style can be had on a shoestring, Woodleigh's house starts with wonderful, wood-clad Northwest bones and continues with an artist's vision. Handcrafted furnishings, strong colors, and the art of family and friends create a welcoming sanctuary. "I love to come home," she says. "It's like jeans that have faded naturally. It's not been acid-washed."

RIGHT *The bedroom has a view of Woodleigh's flower and vegetable garden. The deep red-orange painting is by her father, Earl Hubbard.* LEFT *A cruciform wall of windows makes the perfect spot in the living area for the artist's workspace. Weather permitting, she works outside.* BELOW *A junk-shop pie safe became a folk-art treasure under the artist's spell. She also made the painting above and the ceramics that flank the cupboard.*

Will and Beth Hathaway's Portland Dome

Will Hathaway stands in the middle of his "elegant cave," the ground-hugging, curvilinear home it took a decade for his family to build, waves his arms about, and raves about dome power. "Dome means domicile. We were meant to stand and sweep our arms about and not knock something over or hit a corner and get hurt!"

The Hathaways' honeymoon was a harbinger of things to come. Beth Hathaway watched her husband make a kingdom of round castles in the Carmel-by-the-Sea sands. She joined in his enthusiasm for rounded shapes. Decades later, they built a dome to inhabit, modeled from their favorite material, rocks.

Beth is a painter, Will an industrial designer and formerly the director of a Portland-area art center. They began the cave project in 1977 from their own design using friend and engineer Alan Gaylord's drawings. The intention was to build a sculptural cave on a hillside lot without cutting away the hill but by terracing the house into the slope.

"Our principal concern was living in harmony with the surrounding environment," says Will. "Then it was our sanity," adds Beth.

The thirteen-year project was a family affair from the first shovelful of soil. Beth sprayed sixteen tons of plaster inside to give the cave the appearance of wet sand, then spent eight months sanding the plaster to give the walls smooth, continuous curves. Will sprayed the exterior with shotcrete, a cement concrete mixed with small aggregate, occasionally overloading the lath and in the process covering a salesman, plants, and a neighbor's garage. Their sons learned to count by earning a nickel for every cut of rebar they carried.

The result is an oddly beautiful organic-looking structure that blends the architectural styles of Taos, New Mexico, pueblos, the stone farmhouses of southern France, and the cave dwellings of some native tribes. Cells of rooms swirl off the sunroom entry. Light pours in from the string of openings funneled into the ceiling from the roof, spilling out in a primal glow. Every room but the bath has an outside view.

The couple brought their environmental concerns to the interior details, using recycled materials whenever possible. Will carved a

ABOVE *A concrete skin was the most logical material for the curvilinear cave because of its plasticity, durability, and strength.* RIGHT *The roof "lips" hold soil on the roof, making the home partly subterranean and encouraging a mystery garden. The glass tops allow light to filter through.* FAR RIGHT *A curved hallway leads off in a calligraphic-like swirl to the cell-like chambers that make up the rest of the house. Doors are recycled from a Portland commercial building.*

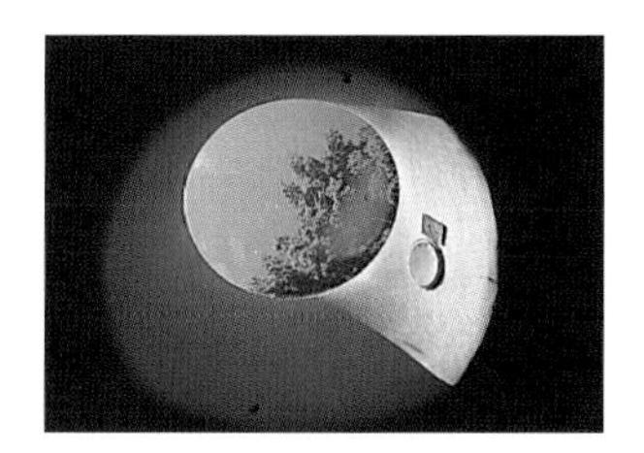

ABOVE *A fragment of nature from the rooftop garden encroaches onto one of the light "cells" cut into the dome's ceiling.* RIGHT *The great room is where the couple spend most of their time, "living happily without a ninety-degree angle in sight," says Will.* LEFT *A sitting room is lit from a sky well above. Will Hathaway's wood sculpture,* Stick 'Em Up, *is in the foreground.*

wooden chair from a felled tree on the site. A stairway banister is a peeled branch from one of their trees. The kitchen's cabinets are stone-colored laminate covers from old computer disk-drive equipment dug from a dumpster in the nearby silicone forest. The arched doors were salvaged from a demolished Portland office building, their rounded shapes proving irresistible to the couple.

The Hathaways hold workshops on organic design at their home and entertain the endless philosophical questions of art and architecture students who share the couple's intrigue for domes. Their two sons are another story. Although grown and gone, they reportedly still flinch at the sight of concrete.

Margie and Arthur Erickson's Portland House

Margie and Arthur Erickson literally coaxed their 1926 English-style stucco house back to life. The grounds were in the clutches of blackberry bushes; the interiors were a shambles. Patiently restored over a decade's time, the gardens now grandstand through the kitchen window, and the interiors reveal the owners' passion for fine and folk art and for legendary dinner parties.

The spirit of organized clutter pervades. Guests don't walk through a room; they navigate. The Ericksons have combined Native American and Eskimo artifacts, primitive and folk art, antique and Arts and Crafts-style furniture in the subconscious manner of an I Ching toss. A few lighthearted objects, such as the Adam's apple of an unknown donor and a walrus with poor taste in neckties also show up in the melange.

Arthur runs the couple's Portland gallery of native ethnographic art and antiquities. Margie restores native artifacts. Many of the ethnic pieces—important ceremonial masks, baskets, beaded bags, and textiles—make it home to mix with Margie's collection of bears. Bear gavels, stuffed bears, bear tables, bear lamps, bear sculptures—even a bear cleverly disguised as a rabbit are ubiquitous—giving the house a frontier vigor and sense of animation.

As serious as her bear fetish is Margie's love of cooking. A recent kitchen remodel has enabled her culinary interest to become pure passion. Portland architect Richard Brown, the couple's friend and someone who knows the pleasure of breaking bread at their table, fleshed out Margie's ideas. "Richard had respect for the architecture of the house," says Margie. "He modernized the kitchen without pulling the house from its era."

Margie wanted a kitchen with both an elegant and handcrafted look. The architect emphasized details from the Arts and Crafts period, incorporating features such as smooth drawer faces with recessed panels, split by decorative vertical divides.

Though small, the kitchen functions with great efficiency; there are no more than three steps separating sink, stove, and refrigerator.

ABOVE *The stucco-clad English cottage in Portland's west hills was lovingly restored inch by inch.* FAR LEFT *One man's trash is another man's folk art. The walrus was tossed out in someone's backyard garbage. Now he greets guests. The early Mickey Mouse sits on a parquet folk art stand made from inlaid plywood. The beaded snake on the wall is from Nigeria. The Ericksons found the handmade chair in an eastern Oregon antique shop.*

ABOVE *A lacquer tray holds early-nineteenth-century Eskimo pieces. Above, a miniature mask from the same period rests in the hollow of an Arts and Crafts lamp.* RIGHT *Margie has restored the beaded bags that hang on the wall above the antique cherry wood table. The bag hanging directly over the chair is a cornhusker's bag. The bookends and Indian baskets are but a fraction of the couple's folk art treasures.* FAR RIGHT *The secret of a successful Northwest-style dinner party? Fresh, regional food such as salmon, mussels, chanterelles, apple pie, and herbs and vegetables just plucked from the garden. "The most important thing is interaction," says Margie. "I'm likely to grab guests and say 'here, chop this.' "*

"A sense of scale was critical to this kitchen," says the architect. "It's a cozy space that encourages intimacy and conversation."

The white wood cabinets *look* handmade rather than manufactured, the glass-front cupboards reveal collections of pottery and art, and the Brazilian cherry wood floor warms the space. Margie loved the stainless look but didn't want a high-tech feel. Mixing stainless steel and African bloodwood softened the look. A new convection oven gives the 1932 stove an occasional day off. Saving space, deep drawers replaced cupboards for large pots and pans. The proverbial icing on the cake, however, is the wooden high-backed booth, squeezed into an alcove. The booth's backs and seats serve as additional storage.

Now the kitchen gets a true chef's workout—as the heart, soul, and muscle of the couple's legendary social repasts.

BIBLIOGRAPHY

Aira, Cesar. *Argentina: The Great Estancias*. New York: Rizzoli, 1995.

Allan, Lois. *Contemporary Art in the Northwest*. Australia: Craftsman House, 1995.

Ambrose, Stephen E. *Undaunted Courage*. New York: Touchstone, 1996.

Bailey, Lee. *Long Weekends: Recipes for Good Food and Easy Living*. New York: Clarkson Potter, 1994.

Bosker, Gideon, and Lena Lencek. *Frozen Music: A History of Portland Architecture*. Portland, OR: Western Imprints, the Press of the Oregon Historical Society, 1985.

Brewster, David, and Stephanie Irving. *Northwest Best Places*. Seattle, WA: Sasquatch Books, 1994–95.

Calloway, Stephen, and Elizabeth Cromley. *Elements of Style*. New York: Simon and Schuster, 1991.

Clark, Rosalind. *Architecture: Oregon Style*. Portland, OR: Professional Book Center, 1983.

Cottrell Houle, Marcy. *One City's Wilderness: Portland's Forest Park*. Portland, OR: Oregon Historical Society, 1988.

Espy, Willard R. *Oysterville: Road to Grandpa's Village*. Seattle, WA: University of Washington Press, 1992.

Hoppen, Kelly. *East Meets West*. New York: Rizzoli, 1997.

Humphrey, Linda, and Fred Albert. *American Design: The Northwest*. New York: Bantam Books, 1989.

Koren, Leonard. *Wabi-Sabi for Artists, Designers, Poets & Philosophers*. Berkeley, CA: Stone Bridge Press, 1994.

Kreisman, Lawrence. *Historic Preservation in Seattle*. Seattle, WA: Historic Seattle Preservation and Development Authority, 1985.

Norse, Elliott. *Ancient Forests of the Pacific Northwest*. Washington, D.C.: Island Press, 1990.

Saenz Quesada, Maria. *Estancias: The Great Houses and Ranches of Argentina*. New York: Abbeville, 1992.

Slesin, Suzanne, Stafford Cliff, and Daniel Rozensztroch. *Japanese Style*. New York: Clarkson N. Potter, 1987.

Vaughan, Thomas, and Virginia Guest Ferriday. *Space, Style and Structure: Building in Northwest America*. Portland, OR: Oregon Historical Society, 1974.

Rain is not the only phenomenon gracing the Pacific Northwest. Style, in its myriad manifestations, abounds, and often at bargain prices. We have a lot to discover, especially in the realm of antiques, recycled retro classics, elegant objets, and fine crafts and art. Browsing the region can yield more treasures than those uncovered by the original gold seekers, fur traders, land barons, and gamblers. Take time for coffee breaks (a coffee bar will be conveniently located at approximately every point of fatigue) and scour the inspiring and unexpectedly eclectic shopping scene. The following listing represents only a sampling of the more unique shops the Northwest has to offer.

Antiques

ANTIQUES AT PIKE PLACE
92 STEWART ST.
SEATTLE, WA 98101
206-441-9643

Everything from Victorian to Art Deco. An eclectic selection of accessories ranges from chandeliers to unique items such as tin paneling.

BOGART BREMMER & BRADLEY ANTIQUES
8000 FIFTEENTH AVE. N.W.
SEATTLE, WA 98117
206-783-7333

A dazzling selection of restored authentic lighting from 1850 to 1950. Also fine American antique furnishings in oak, mahogany, and walnut.

GERALDINE'S ANTIQUES
2772 N.W. THURMAN ST.
PORTLAND, OR 97210
503-295-5911

French, French Canadian, English, and American period furniture, architectural fragments, and liturgical elements.

JADESTONE GALLERY
10922 N.E. ST. JOHNS RD.
VANCOUVER, WA 98686
360-573-2580

3200 S.E. HIGHWAY 101
LINCOLN CITY, OREGON 97367
541-996-2580

Full historical representation of Chinese art, antiques, and antiquities, including early jade implements and tomb pieces. Eighteenth and nineteenth-century American and European zoological and botanical prints.

KAGEDO JAPANESE ART
520 FIRST AVE. S.
SEATTLE, WA 98104
206-467-9077

High-end Japanese furnishings, folk art, and antiques, including merchant chests (choubadansu), *clothing storage chests, stone garden pieces, metalwork, lacquerware, and textiles including period kimono and* Ainu *robes.*

PARTNERS IN TIME
1332 SIXTH AVE.
SEATTLE, WA 98101
206-623-4218

1313 W. BURNSIDE
PORTLAND, OR 97201
503-228-6299

Large space filled with nineteenth-century European pine, Japanese tansu, *porcelain and lacquerware, Pakistani and Turkish primitives and antiques, as well as a full line of bedding, table linens, bath and garden gifts, and accessories.*

PELAYO
7601 GREENWOOD AVE. N.
SEATTLE, WA 98103
206-789-1999

8421 GREENWOOD AVE. N.
SEATTLE, WA 98103
206-789-1333

Russian icons, Royal Copenhagen china, a huge inventory of country pine, and eighteenth- and nineteenth-century Scandinavian, Eastern European, and English furniture.

THREE MONKEYS
803 N.W. TWENTY-THIRD AVE.
PORTLAND, OR 97210
503-222-9894

THREE MORE MONKEYS
817 N.W. TWENTY-THIRD AVE.
PORTLAND, OR 97210
503-222-5802

Owners raid old estates in Palm Springs and return with retro treasures from grand to grand kitsch.

DAVID WEATHERFORD ANTIQUES AND INTERIORS
133 FOURTEENTH AVE. E.
SEATTLE, WA 98112
206-329-6533

Asian porcelain and art and a wide selection of period English and French furnishings and accessories.

JEAN WILLIAMS ANTIQUES
115 S. JACKSON ST.
SEATTLE, WA 98104
206-622-1110

Fine antiques including eighteenth- and nineteenth-century French, English, and American furniture. Accessories range from porcelain boxes, marble urns, and unusual candlesticks to garden stone and statuary.

X DYNASTY
1906 POST ALLEY
HISTORIC PIKE PLACE MARKET
SEATTLE, WA 98101
206-269-0546

Chinese antiques including armoires, cabinets, chairs, and elaborately carved wooden doors with cast-iron fixtures. Accessories include wedding baskets, wooden kitchen items, and food and wine containers.

Fabulous Furnishings, Accessories, and Objets for Home and Garden

ASIA AMERICA
79 S.E. TAYLOR
PORTLAND, OR 97214
503-230-9322

Huge warehouse stocked with eighteenth- and nineteenth-century Chinese imports, North African British colonial furniture, and garden vessels with unusual glazes from Vietnam.

CURRENT
1201 WESTERN AVE.
SEATTLE, WA 98101
206-622-2433

Contemporary Italian- and European-designed furnishings and European lighting and accessories.

DEL-TEET
10308 N.E. TENTH ST.
BELLEVUE, WA 98004
425-462-5400

Classic contemporary furnishings and accessories with an Asian influence. Huge selection of elegant and primitive tansu chests. Fabulous lamps, carpets, fabrics.

DELUXE JUNK
3518 FREMONT PL. N.
SEATTLE, WA 98103
206-634-2733

Recycled modern-era classics.

DESIGN WITHIN REACH
1200 N.W. EVERETT ST.
PORTLAND, OR 97209
503-220-0200

The best of modern design and accessories including unique lighting at affordable prices. Noguchi, Bendtsen, Nelson, Eames, van der Rohe, Le Corbusier, and much more. Friendly staff knows how to pull a stunning look together.

THE GARDEN ROOM
1006 HARRIS AVE., STE. 120
BELLINGHAM, WA 98225
360-734-9949

Stone, wood, bamboo, clay, and lacquer garden accessories from China, Japan, Indonesia, and other exotic locales. Specializing in unusual pots and utilitarian vessels.

HIP
1829 N.W. TWENTY-FIFTH AVE.
PORTLAND, OR 97210
503-225-5017

Urban contemporary furnishings and accessories for office and home in mid-range prices. Unique European imports and American pieces with a youthful edge and comfortable feel.

ITAL INTERIORS INC.
1028 MAINLAND
VANCOUVER, B.C.
CANADA V6B 2T4
604-685-0037

High-end architecturally designed contemporary Italian and Spanish furniture and accessories.

J. D. MADISON RUG AND HOME CO.
1307 N.W. GLISAN
PORTLAND, OR 97210
503-827-6037

Northwest transitional contemporary furniture with Asian undertones. Pure, simple geometric forms in tables, chairs, carpets, and candles.

KASALA
1505 WESTERN AVE.
SEATTLE, WA 98101
206-623-7795

Eclectic assemblage of ultramodern and ultrachic furnishings and accessories from furnishings to minutiae.

MASINS FINE FURNITURE
220 SECOND AVE. S.
SEATTLE, WA 98104
206-622-5606

Enormous selection of contemporary and traditional furnishings, including craftsman style, for the home. Marge Carson, McGuire, Karges, Stickley, Ralph Lauren, and much more. Decorative accessories, antiques, and fine art. Creative and knowledgeable staff.

NORTHWEST FINE FURNISHINGS
919 RIVERSIDE DR.
MT. VERNON, WA 98273
360-424-8455

Unusual contemporary furniture, including leather pieces. Also bookshelves, curios, lamps.

PARKER FURNITURE
10375 S.W. BEAVERTON-HILLSDALE HWY.
BEAVERTON, OR 97005
503-644-0155

Wide selection of traditional and contemporary furnishings, lots of leather, rugs, and accessories. Huge showroom and expert staff. Lines include Stickley, Henredon, Century, Marge Carson, much more.

P. H. REED
1100 N.W. GLISAN
PORTLAND, OR 97209
503-274-7080

Clean, classic contemporary furnishings and lighting using stone, wicker, concrete, sandblasted glass, and aluminum. Many pieces designed by local artists.

ROCKY MOUNTAIN TIMBER PRODUCTS
P.O. BOX 1477
SISTERS, OR 97759
541-549-1322

Rustic, natural-form furniture and architectural accents including large juniper-carved furnishings and accessories.

SEATTLE DESIGN CENTER
5701 SIXTH AVE. S.
SEATTLE, WA 98108
206-762-1200

Open to the public Monday–Friday, 12:00–5:00 p.m.

URBINO
638 N.W. TWENTY-THIRD AVE.
PORTLAND, OR 97210
503-220-4194

Contemporary and antique European furnishings, pottery, dinnerware, picture frames, jewelry, altar candles, gifts.

Art and Craft Galleries

BULLSEYE CONNECTION
1308 N.W. EVERETT ST.
PORTLAND, OR 97209
503-227-2797

Northwest Regional and international contemporary blown and cast glass. Architectural applications.

BUTTERS GALLERY LTD.
520 N.W. DAVIS
PORTLAND, OR 97210
800-544-9171

Emerging and leading Northwest artists and international artists with an emphasis on contemporary abstract art.

CHIHULY INC.
509 N.E. NORTHLAKE WY.
SEATTLE, WA 98105
206-632-8707

Dedicated to the internationally acclaimed icon of Northwest glass, Dale Chihuly.

CONTEMPORARY CRAFTS GALLERY
3934 S.W. CORBETT AVE.
PORTLAND, OR 97201
503-223-2654

Oldest nonprofit crafts gallery in the region, featuring regional works in clay, glass, wood, and metal as well as textiles, jewelry, and garden art.

CURIOS-CITY
3851 MAIN ST.
VANCOUVER, B.C.
CANADA V5V 3P1
604-876-0900

North American Indian masks, totems, tribal pieces, buffalo blankets, and Northwest coastal paintings.

EARTHENWORKS
713 FIRST ST.
LA CONNER, WA 98257
360-466-4422

More than three hundred American craft artists, including leading Northwest craftspeople. Large selection of art glass, jewelry, pottery, clothing, sculpture, and original paintings.

FOSTER/WHITE GALLERY
1420 FIFTH AVE.
SEATTLE, WA 98101
206-340-8025

123 S. JACKSON ST.
SEATTLE, WA 98104
206-622-2833

126 CENTRAL WY.
KIRKLAND, WA 98033
425-822-2305

Wide selection of sculpture, ceramics, paintings, prints, and glassware. Featuring leading glass artists, including Dale Chihuly. Also features Northwest masters Morris Graves, Mark Tobey, George Tsutakawa, and Kenneth Callahan.

LINDA HODGES GALLERY
410 OCCIDENTAL AVE. S.
SEATTLE, WA 98104
206-624-3034

Specializing in contemporary Northwest paintings by regional artists.

HOFFMAN GALLERY
OREGON COLLEGE OF ART AND CRAFT
8245 S.W. BARNES RD.
PORTLAND, OR 97225
503-297-5544

Monthly exhibitions featuring students' work in pottery, photography, textiles, wood, glass, and jewelry are featured in the gallery. Sales gallery carries work by Northwest artists.

MARK WOOLLEY GALLERY
120 N.W. NINTH ST.,
SUITE 210
PORTLAND, OR 97209
503-224-5475

Wide selection of regional artists featuring avant garde works, some outsider art, sculpture and photography. Owner a zealous patron to burgeoning artists and many receive their first show at this fine gallery.

GREG KUCERA GALLERY
212 THIRD AVE. S.
SEATTLE, WA 98104
206-624-0770

Contemporary paintings, fine prints, sculpture, and works on paper by leading regional and national artists.

ELIZABETH LEACH GALLERY
207 S.W. PINE
PORTLAND, OR 97204
503-224-0521

Specializing in Northwest contemporary artists and emerging artists from the region.

NORTHWEST CRAFT CENTER AND GALLERY
SEATTLE CENTER
SEATTLE, WA 98103
206-728-1555

Artisan-made one-of-a-kind pieces, including woodcraft, jewelry, pottery, and glass.

LAURA RUSSO GALLERY
805 N.W. TWENTY-FIRST ST.
PORTLAND, OR 97209
503-226-2754

Emerging and established Northwest contemporary artists, including

Northwest masters Michele Russo and Sally Haley. Also features well-known national and international contemporary painters.

TWIST
30 N.W. TWENTY-THIRD PL.
PORTLAND, OR 97210
503-224-0334

National and regional high-end crafts and art, including fine jewelry, pottery, unusual handcrafted furnishings, and accessories.

UNO LANGMANN LTD.
2117 GRANVILLE
VANCOUVER, B.C.
CANADA V6H 3E9
604-736-8825

High-end elegant European and North American paintings from the eighteenth, nineteenth, and early twentieth centuries, as well as a selection of antique furnishings, silver, and objets d'art.

Starting Places and Finishing Touches

ANN GARDNER
4136 MERIDIAN AVE. N.
SEATTLE, WA 98103
206-547-8002

Seattle artist specializing in printmaking and sculpture with emphasis on architectural applications, including glass mosaic.

HIPPO HARDWARE AND TRADING COMPANY
1040 EAST BURNSIDE
PORTLAND, OR 97214
503-231-1444

New, used, and restored lighting, plumbing fixtures, and salvaged architectural details, including doors, windows, and hardware.

MUD PIE STUDIOS
4225 S.W. ALFRED ST.
PORTLAND, OR 97219
503-493-2668

Specializing in artistic concrete works for home and garden. Concrete countertops for kitchen and bath. Tables, tiles, garden benches in Northwest/ Asian style with an organic look and feel. Incorporation of natural stones, bamboo, copper, and other elements in many designs.

NORTHWEST SOCIETY OF INTERIOR DESIGNERS (NWSID)
SEATTLE DESIGN CENTER
5701 SIXTH AVE. S., STE. 407
SEATTLE, WA 98108
206-763-8799

DOROTHY A. PAYTON
ORGANIZATIONAL AND
BUILDING ECOLOGY
FENG SHUI PRACTITIONER
P.O. BOX 82470
PORTLAND, OR 97282
503-236-2141

Focusing on the environmental, physical, and spiritual aspects of space planning, including feng shui.

REJUVENATION LAMP AND FIXTURE COMPANY
1100 S.E. GRAND AVE.
PORTLAND, OR 97214
503-231-1900

Fine reproduction lighting, from craftsman to Modern to Victorian atomic-age American.

ANN SACKS TILEWORKS
115 STEWART ST.
SEATTLE, WA 98101
206-441-8917

Unique artist-designed handcrafted tiles and natural stone.

R. WAGNER COMPANY
205 N.W. TENTH ST.
PORTLAND, OR 97209
503-224-7036

Design and execution of antique reproductions, architectural art, hand-painted interior and exterior surface applications.

INDEX